URBAN GUN DOGS

Doug!
Thanks "Purdy Boy"!
Thanks that training!
Keep up that training
and don't think so much!!
Just do!! Love you man!

Benjamin Richleau

URBAN GUN DOGS

Training Flushing Dogs for Home and Field

Anthony Z. Roettger and Benjamin H. Schleider III

THE WRITERS' COLLECTIVE 🎣 Cranston, Rhode Island

Independent Books for Indpendent Readers

Urban Gun Dogs

© 2005 Anthony Z. Roettger and Benjamin H. Schleider III

Cover Design: Barbara Hodge
Cover Photo: Catharine Schleider
Book Design: Day to Day Enterprises
Photography: Anthony Z. Roettger and Benjamin H. Schleider III

ISBN: 1-59411-050-6

Library of Congress Control Number: 2004095939

Printed in the United States of America
10 9 8 7 6 5 4 3 2 1

Published by The Writers' Collective ✦ Cranston, Rhode Island

TABLE OF CONTENTS

PREFACE

Ever since I was very, very young, dog training has never been far from my thoughts. As a boy, I dreamed incessantly of owning a spaniel, retriever, or pointing dog over which I would shoot grouse and pheasants native to rural Minnesota. However, no matter how often I badgered my poor, overworked parents, I always lost the battle for a dog. And to this day I am not certain why. Frustrated early on in my quest for a hunting dog, I gravitated toward quarter horses. For some reason, my parents apparently were under the mistaken impression that horses were easier to maintain. My involvement with horses spanned more than ten years, and during that period, I managed to make sufficient money to afford a car and college. I worked part time in the evenings until I graduated, and then was lucky enough to land a full time job as a tool designer and CNC programmer.

Two months after I graduated, I found the dog I had been seeking. This dog was to be the realization of all of those unfulfilled youthful dreams–the perfect companion for home and field. In procuring my dream dog, I did what many first time buyers do. Not knowing any better, I pulled out the Sunday newspaper, found an ad for English springer spaniel puppies, took a look at the litter, and selected a female puppy that looked the best. After all the experience training quarter horses, my expectation for the relationship between my newfound friend and me was that, after only a few growing pains, we would become a close-knit team, acting as one in the field, in our search for elusive game birds. Reality was far, far different; she became an absolute tyrant.

One particularly vivid memory is indelibly etched into my brain. Shortly after I acquired my new bundle of puppy joy, I happened to be watching my grandparents' Minnesota home for the winter. In rapid succession, Lady tore up my grandmother's carefully selected and lovingly maintained porcelain and hand crafted knick knacks (the little crocheted thing with eyes that she used to cover the "extra" roll of toilet paper in the bathroom retained only half an eye and no nose). My sweet grandmother, holding her consternation to her grave, never did mention the broken items, although I suspect she must have made a few observations to my grandfather after Lady and I departed. Lady then moved to quickly destroy a new pair of hunting boots and jacket, mess the carpet and floor, tear up the bed linens, and generally cause chaos on a grand scale. She whined incessantly at night, so much so that I had to let her sleep with me for a week or so. At that point, I decided to buy a crate and then proceeded to "fix" my grandmothers things. This was not the roaring start I had envisioned.

There were, however, some bright spots. Lady dearly loved to find and carry things in her mouth, and took readily to flushing and retrieving upland game birds. Despite Lady's idiosyncrasies, I was confidant that she would at least make a fairly good hunting dog. That was until Lady encountered mallard ducks at our first of many, many Hunt Tests. Unbeknownst to me, Lady hated ducks and for many years this has been the bird of choice in Minnesota AKC Hunt Tests. In our training sessions, we utilized pigeons, pheasants, and quail, but because of the cost and availability of ducks we had never trained with them. It never dawned on me that Lady would have any problems with ducks, but in her first Junior Hunter test, she absolutely refused to have anything to do with mallards (or any other kind of duck for that matter).

After two straight years and thirteen unsuccessful attempts, Lady finally received her first Junior Hunter ribbon and qualifying score–

a testament to our collective perseverance. I am certain that this is some sort of record in the state of Minnesota and perhaps nationwide. Once she had received that first qualifying score, Lady quickly in turn obtained her Junior Hunter and Senior Hunter titles as a steady to flush dog. She then went on to Master Hunter level. Although Lady did pick up some qualifying legs on her Master Hunter title, she never finished the title. Her abject dislike of ducks combined with her natural intelligence and mischievous personality created an obstacle neither of us could overcome. She was a smart dog and would conveniently refuse or forget how to do the water blind. She learned that I could not discipline her at these events while under the eyes of the judges, so she would go part way into the water, stop, turn, and look at me. She absolutely refused to go any further into the pond, although she was an excellent swimmer. I could swear that she actually gave me a little smile along with a sparkling glint in her eye as she stood there defying my attempts to get her to swim the forty some odd yards to the opposite shore and make the retrieve. It was in this less than glory-covered fashion that I embarked upon my career as a gun dog trainer.

After years of training Lady, I finally got a second dog. The new dog was a small black English cocker spaniel–my first introduction to Cockers. As Keith Erlandson puts it, "it is a well known fact that the old gentleman from the Nether regions is a keen shooting man and there he shoots, over a pack of Cockers...black Cockers, with live embers for eyes! Each one runs and gives tongue and all bite their birds like fury. Every now and then their owner sends his worst stud dog to earth, to mate a few bitches, thus ensuring that his chosen qualities are not lost." That is the dog I got, and what a treat Sky still is today. Possessed of an innate talent combined with immense power all fused in a compact, thirty-four pound package, Sky was the genesis of my career as a professional trainer of flushing gun dogs.

I decided early on that flushing dogs in general and spaniels in particular were my forte. I once undertook to train a pointer, and she became one of the best flushing dogs I have ever trained. With Sky I began to experience all the joys, so unlike the trials and tribulations of Lady, that owning a top-notch flushing spaniel can bring. It was also through training gun dogs and participating in hunt tests that I met my wife, partner, and best friend, Bethann–both of us having long since dedicated ourselves to the world of gun dogs. As we started our new lives together, increasingly we were asked by friends and acquaintances to train their dogs. They have always been the rock upon which we have rested.

But perhaps the primary impetus for me to move to the professional ranks came from Paul McGagh, and to this day I am not certain if he realizes the impact he has had on my life. I had watched Paul on ESPN Outdoors on Saturday mornings putting his dogs through their paces, and winning consistently on the highly competitive field trial circuit. Later, we happened to meet at a Field Trial and discovered a mutual common interest. Sky, my English cocker, had been sired by one of Paul's Field Champions. We struck up a fast friendship. Bethann and I subsequently purchased a couple of dogs from him and one day he said, in his delightful, warm British accent, "Tony, have you ever thought of becoming a "Professional?" At first I scoffed at the idea. But later, after much reflection and discussions with Bethann on the proposition, I began to warm to the idea. Ultimately I took the plunge. The same week I turned professional, our Roettger Ridge Kennel had its first two clients.

Successes in Hunt Tests and Field Trials, as well as word of mouth have fueled our client base, and our dog training program has continued expand. Not long ago there was a magazine article on Roettger Ridge and our cockers in *Bird Dog & Retriever News*. Shortly thereafter, Jerry Thoms published an article in *Gun Dog Magazine* on our cocker program. The past few years have been a dream come true, and both Bethann and I are genuinely grateful to our many friends and family for the support they have given us in launching Roettger Ridge Kennel.

Gun dog training, in the main, is a very dirty job. It can be frustrating, disappointing, and time consuming, but it has its moments of high excitement, glamour, and reward. Not long ago, Bethann and I saw the movie "The Rookie" a true story about Jimmy Morris, a middle-aged, worn out professional pitcher turned high school coach, whose injured arm magically heals giving Morris his shot at the major leagues. While still in the minors, Morris, played by actor Dennis Quaid, starts to think he will never make the major leagues. He has a minor revelation over a beer between games when he witnesses a little league game in progress across the street. He heads back to the locker room with a smile on his face and says to another player, "You know what we get to do today? We get to play Baseball." I know exactly how Morris felt. Whenever I get down and out a bit, I always remember that I get to go out and play with dogs everyday–something that I dearly love.

Happy training,
Tony Roettger

INTRODUCTION

Dogs are the sirens of the world of creatures. They worm their way into our heart as puppies; as they grow older, dogs become members of your families, confidants, partners, and friends. These devious creatures gain our hearts, and then when they grow old before our very eyes, just as quickly break them when they pass from this world. One is left cast upon the rocks of emotion time and again. Why then do we want them? What compels a person continually to place his or her heart in jeopardy?

Millennia ago, when the first man found a wolf cub, brought it to his campfire, domesticated it, and later on hunted with it, a bond was formed that thousands of years of human and canine breeding has re-enforced. It starts with the smell of puppy breath, grows with that trusting warmth of their eyes, and lasts through the years of companionship, old age, and death. If you think this is a sappy, sentimental way in which to begin a book about gun dog training, you are perhaps correct, and perhaps you really should not be in the gun dog training business. If you are foolish enough to embrace these beliefs and go down that path, this book is for you.

Tony and Bethann Roettger asked me to write this introduction, because I am exactly the type of person for whom this book is designed–a perfect combination of a naïve, beginning dog trainer and handler living in an urban environment–a true guinea pig of the first order. The genesis of this book actually was a telephone conversation in September of 2000, which in turn was the result of a prolonged session of web surfing and research in search of a hunting dog. After a hiatus of more than twenty plus years, I had decided to get back into bird hunting.

As a youth, I shot doves and quail in central Texas during those incredibly long, hot, and humid fall hunting seasons in the mid-1960s peppered with heavy dove migrations, brilliant sunsets, and Texas A&M football games on the radio. I recall one particular hunt when I consumed a six-pack of Dr. Pepper while listening to the 1967 Texas A&M-Texas Tech football game sitting in a Ford station wagon. I was alternatively smothering when the windows were up, and being eaten alive by mosquitoes when the windows were rolled down. During radio commercials I reflected on the doves I had shot during the day and the beauty of it all. My dad concentrated on consuming Lone Star beer and swapping hunting stories with his business partners a hundred feet away in a two story, restored 1840s Texas farmhouse complete with a dog trot. It was a long trek back for me; a path many people with my background–a combination of a suburban and somewhat rural upbringing–have taken over the years.

During the course of my career, Door, my long-suffering wife of twenty-seven years, and I had lived in Germany during post-Vietnam military service–the nation must indeed count itself fortunate that no Soviet invasion occurred on my watch as a field artillery second lieutenant stationed near Nuremberg. We spent many years living a hand-to-mouth existence on the GI Bill in graduate school, and endured a career of constant relocation and international travel owing to my job as a business development professional with a large defense contractor. As I inexorably approached the transition point of middle age, I began to think about returning to that yesteryear of my youth– bird hunting. This time, however, I wanted it all–game birds and a dog with which to hunt them.

My vision flowed in the main from the superb short stories and idyllic bird hunting expeditions detailed in such periodicals as *Sporting*

Classics, Shooting Sportsman, The Upland Almanac, and *Gray's Sporting Journal*. I pictured myself in the company of a superbly trained English springer spaniel (I relatively early on settled on springers for no other reason than I thought they looked really good). It was there that research started. After multiple uncoordinated forays into cyber space, I actually developed a plan. I would formulate a list of breeders offering puppies, email them to assess their availability, conduct a series of telephone interviews, and decide on the dog. I had not the foggiest idea how to train a dog for bird hunting, so I was prepared to gamble; I would ask the breeder to raise the dog as his own for a year in his house and provide initial gun dog training. Since Door's approval of the dog procurement plan rested upon me obtaining a female springer fully housebroken with some semblance of obedience training under her belt, I was forced down the path of obtaining a started dog.

I received six replies to my cry for help, and interviewed all six breeders telephonically. When I asked the tough question of the first five: "Would you raise her in the house for a year and start her as a bird dog." The replies I received ranged from, "Gee, I don't think we do it that way," to a polite form of "You need to have your head examined." After several of these interchanges, my frustration factor was getting pretty high; that is when I found Tony and Bethann Roettger who were headquartered in perhaps one of the most Nordic cities of the United States–North Branch, Minnesota, not far from the twin cities. Tony and Bethann were not only willing to accept the challenge of raising a puppy in their home and starting her on the path to becoming a fully finished bird dog, but were prepared to train me as well. The depth of my lack of knowledge was apparent during the first telephone conversation, when I asked the question, "How old are springers when they learn to point?"

Tony and Bethann have extensive experience in raising and training hunting dogs of all types. Their particular focus has been on field-bred English springer spaniels and English cocker spaniels. Any given weekend (or weekday for that matter) will find five to ten dog enthusiasts training at Roettger Ridge Kennels. The spring and fall are given over to field trials and hunt tests; their winters generally include a trip to England to select a few field-bred cockers and springers for return with them to the United States (with a liberal dose of grouse hunting and single malt Scotch sprinkled in as well).

During the course of our relationship, this patient, over-worked, and dedicated couple has endured every possible question concerning dog training and socialization from me. My three dogs Dixie, a three year old field-bred English springer spaniel, Arwen, an adorably diminutive but spunky field-bred English cocker spaniel, and Jazz, a hard-core field trialing English cocker import from the United Kingdom–all products of the excellent Roettger breeding and training program, are equally at home here in Northern Virginia or in North Branch. Many of the training techniques contained in this book are the result of our mutual experiences. Between us, I think we have digested most if not all of the available books on flushing dog training.

It is our assessment the majority of these books deal superbly with all of the aspects of training a dog to excel in the field, on the field trial circuit, or in hunt tests. Most of these books are written by truly great trainers and handlers who live in beautiful, often very rural, areas of the United States. They live the life I aspire to live some day, training dogs and shooting birds on eighty to one hundred acres with a farmhouse that began life in the mid-1830's. Unfortunately, many of the dog training techniques detailed in these well written manuals are not optimized for what we are increasingly witnessing in gun dog circles as the urban hunter and gun dog owner. This book was born on a very long coast-to-coast flight from Northern Virginia to Washington State with an intermediate stop in Denver to discuss the concept with Tony and Bethann. Its outlines took shape after three glasses of a surprisingly good Merlot on the back of an envelope (no kidding).

The book starts with the premise that urban gun dog owners are, if not now ultimately will be, the principle gun dog owners. They hunt on public land or preserves, participate in field trials, and try their luck and skill in hunt tests. This new breed of gun dog owners is characterized by its zest for the sporting life, love of their dogs, and absence of rural property. The hunting landscape has changed forever in the United States. Extensive urban development and intensive farming techniques have reduced bird populations significantly. No longer do hunters enjoy the ability to gain easy access to private land. Today's hunter is far more likely to live or work in an urban area, hunt either on public land or on private game preserves, travel extensively to hunt, and, if he or she owns a dog, likely not have the luxury of possessing land for dog training or outdoor kennels.

It has become increasingly obvious to us there is a gap in the gun dog training literature that has ignored the plight of the urban gun dog owner. The demands of city dwelling on trainer and dog are such that traditional gun dog training techniques may produce a sound hunting companion, but ignore the training imperatives that assist in adapting a dog for the urban environment. The result is the urban-dwelling amateur must rely upon professional trainers or techniques that will only partially achieve what a gun dog needs to fully adapt to living in today's constrained, crowded, and dangerous urban environments, or require rural property to implement.

It is with this reality in mind that we three undertook to write this book. It focuses on training techniques specifically developed with the urban flushing gun dog owner in mind, but is broadly applicable to all dogs. It draws upon the extensive experiences of Tony and Bethann Roettger in training English springer spaniel and English cocker spaniel gun dogs for field trials, hunt tests, hunting, or just plain fun. The authors have assumed your training time is limited, you have limited access to rural areas, and you must do the bulk of your training alone.

This book is written primarily for the novice gun dog owner (male or female) who is a working stiff. This is the person who rises early to beat the traffic and slogs sleepy-eyed to work, slurping lukewarm coffee from a leaky travel mug while fighting congested highways, fender benders, mean-spirited drivers, and miserable weather. After putting in eight to ten hours shuffling papers, answering phone calls, turning a wrench, or processing claims, our hero climbs into the car, fights an hour's worth of traffic home bleary-eyed to face dinner, kids, and an hour of the latest reality show on television. It requires iron will, immense self-discipline, and often a Herculean effort to get out of the easy chair, put the beer or glass of wine down, and spend a good half an hour to forty-five minutes working with your gun dog.

Today's urban inhabitant is sorely pressed for time, short on energy, and sometimes a little short on patience at the end of a long working day. We have developed an approach to selecting and training gun dogs for the hunter or hunting dog fancier who finds himself or herself in this situation. This approach is novel, because it reduces the amount of training time that requires rural or specialized training facilities. We recognize that to have a fully trained gun dog, however, you will have to find a way to gain access to some rural training facilities or send your dog to a professional breeder/trainer at some point during your training program. The trick for the urban gun dog owner and trainer is to accomplish as much training as possible without these facilities. Our approach is designed around both the time and training facility constraints facing gun dog owners who live in the city.

The authors have day jobs in and around the city. They commute daily from home to work and back again. The Roettgers enjoy that unique blend of an urban and rural lifestyle in the twin cities area of Minnesota. The Schleiders are smack dab in suburbia surrounded by manicured lawns, common areas, and neighbors ready at the drop of a hat to remind you of the leash laws so important to this Northern Virginia suburb of Washington, DC. In short we face all the obstacles you face to owning and training a gun dog in the city.

We also want to make sure, right up front, that our readers are clear on one thing: we are primarily spaniel people with a strong partiality toward retrievers. Not that other dogs, the pointers and some versatile dogs (such as field-bred Airedales) will not make excellent hunting dogs or can be adapted to the urban environment. They do and can. It is our opinion, however, that of all the gun dog breeds, spaniels and retrievers offer perhaps the best mix of size, versatility of game, temperament, retriever instinct, and home adaptability to improve your chances of obtaining a gun dog that is equally at ease in your home or in the field. Retrievers and spaniels especially (to which I am personally partial) excel at hunting upland game–pheasants, grouse, woodcock, quail, chukars, and Hungarian partridge. To a great extent, the more popular retriever breeds recently have overshadowed significantly the spaniel breeds as both house and gun dogs. To be fair to the reader, we do not seek to hide our partiality toward the spaniel breeds, and this book is primarily written with spaniels in mind. We believe that spaniels are extremely talented flushing dogs. They also are superb water retrievers and will do for almost all waterfowl retrieving situations with the exception of extremely cold water. Although the larger of the spaniel breeds can retrieve Canada geese (even a small 25-pound English cocker has been known to fetch downed Canada geese) the heavier waterfowl will probably remain the preserve of Chesapeake Bay and Labrador retrievers.

Pound for pound spaniels are "dogs that do it all," according to John McGonigle in a recent *Gun Dog Magazine* article. It is our belief that spaniels, once extremely popular as gun dogs, have suffered from a lack of publicity. The beauty of spaniels, their strong personal bond with their masters, dynamic flushing style, personality, and downright good looks have made us admittedly a little besotted with them. However, we recognize the there are circumstances in which a spaniel may not be the best choice for an urban dweller. Having laid bare our spaniel biases, we have designed the training techniques outlined in this book to be equally applicable to training retrievers as flushing dogs. It is our hope that urban retriever owners, of which there are certainly very, very many, also will find this book extremely useful in developing a tailored plan designed to turn your field-bred retriever into a solid upland hunting companion, and forgive us our spaniel biases.

Although the techniques outlined in this book are applicable irrespective of the degree of experience of the reader, they are couched more toward the needs of the novice urban gun dog owner. Tony and I hope that you all will enjoy reading this book as much as the authors did writing it, and that it will assist you in obtaining and training a true family and hunting companion. As for me, I have already had my reward last year when Dixie hunted South Dakota with my two sons and me. The boys and the dog did me proud.

Chip Schleider
Great Falls, Virginia

Ch. Noma's Upland Empress, WDX, a true American water spaniel, owner: Brian O'Dell. (Photo by Brian O'Dell).

ONE

The Right Dog for Your Situation

Size and Breed Matters

There is a puzzling array of choices of gun dogs available to the urban hunter today, and it is by no means a simple task to sort through the literature and decide on a dog that fits your particular needs and situation. Should you buy a flushing dog, a pointer, or a retriever? How will the dog adapt to urban life? Will it play gently with small children? Am I able to invite people into my house without fear of my dog attacking them? How will it integrate into my family? And most importantly, will my marriage survive the inevitable strains?

These questions are truly important ones and will influence significantly your choice of breed. Irrespective of your breed choice, there is one essential ingredient to success–*your choice of breeder/trainer*. The choice of breeder is critical if you want both a quality gun dog and an adoring family dog. Gun dogs do not come from a pet store or a neighborhood breeder. In all of the breeds discussed in this book, there is a fairly healthy divide between those dogs bred for the show ring (called conformation in the American Kennel Club parlance, or bench dogs) and those bred for the field. Over the past fifty years, virtually every sporting dog breed has divided into bench and field strains. Despite some heroic attempts to reunify the two and the occasional exceptional dog, the division appears permanent.

Bench-bred and field-bred spaniels at work: bench: Ch. Ramblewoods Crystal Clear SH, owner Tracy & Patty Salzwedel (Photo by Patty Salzwedel); field bred FC Priorsmeadow Yasmin MH, owner Anthony Z. Roettger at the 2003 Cocker Nationals. (Photo by C. Hartman).

English springer spaniels or golden retrievers, for example, bred for the bench look fundamentally different than those bred for the field. Bench dogs have the extreme good looks one associates with the show ring. A field-bred springer or golden will possess far less feathering of the coat, with a concomitant reduction in grooming needs, and have a far greater natural bird finding and retrieving ability than a bench dog. However, they will still be awfully nice to look at. Bench dogs tend be far more available to the prospective dog owner than field-bred dogs. One need merely peruse the local paper's want ads, check with friends, or visit a pet store. To obtain field dogs, the urban hunter must go to a reputable field breeder irrespective of the breed choice. This is not to say that some bench dogs cannot turn into reasonably good hunting dogs with much work, patience, and professional help. However, it is to say that generally field-bred dogs require far less training, have greater natural instincts toward field work, and will generally be hunting much sooner than dogs bred for the bench. They will also make wonderful additions to your family. However, lest the reader believe that the authors are highly prejudiced against show dogs, we must point out that we have seen some nifty field work from dogs not originally bred for the field. Tony's own experiences with his first dog Lady underscore that with hard work and diligence one can accomplish significant feats. If you have not yet made your choice of type of dog, consider a field bred spaniel or retriever; it can make your training tasks easier. If you already have the dog of your dreams, follow the training regime we outline. It can help turn your dog into a solid field performer..

Temperament and intellect, as well as hunting ability, are crucial selection criteria. It is important, we believe, to dispel a myth about field-bred dogs and their ability to adapt to the urban environment right up front. Contrary to many preconceptions, a field-bred spaniel or retriever can make a very good housedog as well as a sound field companion. With a little training, a lot of love and attention, and *a solid match of dog type to your personal situation*, you can have a dog that meets all (or perhaps most) of your requirements. It has been our experience that field-bred spaniels and retrievers tend to be highly intelligent, biddable, and loving companions. They adapt well in most instances to home and field–characteristics that are critical for the urban hunter. Regardless of type, however, all dogs require significant attention.

Selecting the Right Dog

Selecting a dog for the field and suburban environment is a critical step that must be undertaken with you and your spouse as partners. The urban environment is highly demanding–especially if you live in areas that place heavy restrictions on pet ownership, or if both adult members of a household work. The decision to bring a dog into the household must be a family one. To bring home a brand-new puppy in a cardboard carton with the exclamation "Honey, look what I got today. Isn't he cute?" is an approach doomed to failure into today's modern urban household. It may also net you a few nights on the couch.

The best approach starts with a clear idea of the level of training you want your dog to have before you decide on the breed of dog. In today's highly demanding urban life style, it is vital to have an agreement among family members as to the level of training you want the dog to have before you bring him home. This in turn may narrow the choices of breed type. With respect to breed and at the risk of alien-ating some very dear friends who place great stock in their pointing dogs, it is our assessment that flushing dogs, the spaniels and retriev-ers, are perhaps the best suited by style, breeding, and temperament to the urban environment.

Flushing dogs, are among the oldest of the hunting dog breeds. Their original purpose was to flush or "spring" game for falconers be-fore the advent of modern shotguns. Flushing dogs work very close to the hunter through breeding, instinct, and training. In the flushing style, spaniels and retrievers work to "flush" birds from cover within shotgun range of the hunter. A flushing dog hunts perhaps no more than ten to fifteen yards in front of the handler and twenty or so yards to either side as it "quarters" the ground in the classic "windshield wiper" pattern that varies slightly depending upon the direction of the wind. These dogs obtain their scent from the air and the ground, unlike a pointer that takes its scent primarily from the air. Because of the spaniel and retriever scenting style, they cannot cover the same area that pointing dogs are able to cover, but work much closer to the hunter than pointers. This is a direct result of centuries of breeding and a highly developed instinct.

A True Couch Potato.
(Photo by Catharine Schleider).

Because flushing dogs work close to the hunter from instinct, they are gen-erally (not always, unfor-tunately) far less prone to run off from their mas-ters. Their instinctual close working style and loving nature combines with their highly developed retrieving instinct to make them ide-ally suited to the needs of today's urban hunter. Field-bred spaniels and retriev-ers have the ability to stay indoors for extended peri-ods and "turn off" the field while indoors, especially as they mature. They also have that unique ability to "turn on" their bird hunting abilities when they walk out the front door. Flushing dogs also tend to be less rambunctious, especially as they mature.

Pointers, on the other hand, because of their scenting style that takes the scent from the air rather than the ground, tend to range further from the hunter instinctively. They obviously cover more ground, but are much less in the hunter's direct control in their hunting style. They require more land to train on and generally are less aggressive on retrieves than spaniels or retrievers. Many pointers (of course there are exceptions) are relatively high-energy dogs that make the transition to housedogs less readily than the more docile spaniel and retriever breeds. Training pointing dogs to be steady to wing and shot (or "holding a point") requires a lot of training space, many birds, and much time. You can get a young flushing dog working in the field much sooner and without as much training (albeit not steady to wing and shot) as you would need for a young pointer. To be sure, the Brittany is somewhat different than most of the other pointers and has its devotees who live in urban areas. In fairness, however, we must point out the Brittany has only recently departed the spaniel ranks; only within the last decade was the suffix "spaniel" dropped from its AKC breed name. Similarly, one may find "pointing" Labrador retrievers with temperament and handling characteristics similar to the flushing variety. By and large, however, it has been our experience that flushing spaniels and retrievers on the average are better suited for city life and the urban gun dog trainer than pointers.

A dog's size matters significantly for urban owners. City dwelling dictates inhabitants live in constrained spaces. Homes are generally smaller; the yards tend to be under an acre (if they live in single family dwellings with yards), and people have to sometimes drive considerable distances to get from home to recreation facilities, shopping malls, grocery stores, parks, and places of employment. As a rule of thumb for the urban resident, the smaller a dog is, the better. Small dogs require less space in the home and especially in the car. Spaniels and retrievers are well sized for urban hunters.

It is axiomatic amongst professional trainers and dog breeders of the "hunting" type dogs that matching the right field dog to a particular urban situation requires forethought and a clear understanding of dog types and characteristics on the part of all family members. A really good breeder/trainer must be as much of a psychologist as a dog raiser and trainer. The exceptional ones are hard to find and if "Murphy's Law" prevails, likely will be far removed geographically from the prospective buyer. It is almost the rule rather than the exception that the best breeder/trainers for the breed being sought are found 1,000 to 2,000 miles from the prospective urban buyer. It is essential, therefore, the prospective buyer do his or her homework well in advance.

We recommend visiting a kennel to look at puppies, but a decision to buy a dog must be based upon the reputation of the breeder and quality of dogs the kennel has, not the cute, wiggly, and lovable puppy staring you in the face.

Your Breeder/Trainer: Key to Success

Selecting a breeder/trainer is somewhat like shopping for a new home in a city in which you have never lived without the benefit of a real estate agent. This is potentially a foreboding task, one that in past years may have dissuaded the faint of heart. It is far easier now than it has ever been to match up your field dog needs with reputable breeders/trainers capable of meeting those needs.

The internet has become the primary resource for locating, vetting, and obtaining a breeder with the right dog, at the right age, with the right amount of training for your needs. Most well-respected breeders have their own web sites detailing their breed stock, their credentials, and basic information concerning their training programs and dog availability. The web has proven to be a godsend for connecting prospective buyers in one part of the country with breeders in another part of the United States. Other primary sources of information on breeders are the advertising sections of *Gun Dog Magazine*, *Spaniels in the Field*, *Bird Dog & Retriever News* and the websites of breed organizations. The prospective buyer may also wish to consult secondary sources such as *Shooting Sportsman*, *The Upland Almanac*, *The Retriever Journal*, *Sporting Classics*, and *Gray's Sporting Journal*.

We suggest you invest as much time as you need in researching, emailing, and talking to breeders/trainers. Also talk to friends and acquaintances who own gun dogs. It is time well spent. Most really good breeders will want to interview you as much as you interview them. They have a vested interest in ensuring their dogs are well placed with a suitable family. After all, top-notch breeders have a reputation to uphold, and many of them are extremely particular as to whom receives their dogs. It is not unheard of for a reputable breeder to refuse to sell a dog to prospective buyer because the breeder views the buyer as less than committed to training the dog or has concerns about how a buyer might treat a dog. What makes a breeder reputable? Clearly a wall full of ribbons from field trials and hunt tests is one indication. Recommendations from knowledgeable gun dog owners are also a good means to find the right breeder. Visiting field trials and hunt tests and talking to the winners of field trials or "master hunter" owners in the case of the hunt test is a good start. An interview of more than one prospective breeder is essential. In any case, a prospective gun dog owner living in the city should seek a breeder that also is a trainer, and one with whom the prospective owner feels comfortable working.

Before you select your type of breed, we believe that it is extremely important to understand what stage of dog you wish to procure–a puppy, started dog, or finished dog. If you elect to procure a puppy, your choices of breed type, although very important, are less limited. As you progress up the training curve in terms of how trained you want your dog to be before you bring him home, your choices become increasingly more limited. This is simply supply and demand. The more exotic breeds of spaniel or retriever are difficult to find in the United States as puppies. Breeders/trainers, therefore, willing to take a puppy and turn it into a started or finished dog are harder to find. This is not to say that the more rare spaniel and retriever breeds do not make solid, hard working field dogs. They do. However, you will have to invest significantly in time and effort to research these breeds, train them to the level you are seeking, and you may in fact have to wait quite a while before a litter or a highly trained dog becomes available.

Puppies

The most lovable, intoxicating, and delightful animal for those who love dogs is the puppy. I have known the most hardened veteran of dog training and fieldwork to get all misty-eyed, coo, and talk baby

Puppies are Devilish Creatures. (Photos by Tony Roettger, Randy Jahnke and Bob Diehl).

talk when confronted with a litter of spaniel or retriever puppies. These devilish creatures cloud the senses and the judgment. It is a rare person indeed who can sit down with a litter of puppies, play with them, sniff them, let them lick your face, and not buy one.

Despite their charm, the urban buyer must carefully evaluate the pros and cons of procuring a puppy. For those who have never owned a gun dog or had a dog as a pet, the puppy option may not be the best. With a puppy, the new owner will have to start from scratch in training the dog. This means experiencing the trials and tribulations of crate training, basic obedience training, and basic gun dog training. Puppies require attention in prodigious doses. Singles and couples who work should carefully evaluate their personal situations before they elect to buy a puppy. Neglected puppies often develop behavioral problems if left alone for significant periods of time. Naturally, puppies do not possess the control of their bodily functions as compared to more mature dogs–be prepared for accidents.

Having been forewarned, should you elect to go down the path of buying a puppy, be prepared to spend the time necessary to help your new companion develop into a mature gun dog and a solid companion. It is time extremely well spent.

Started dogs

Perhaps one of the best choices the novice can make is to select a started dog, approximately one year old, raised and trained by a professional. Although the standard for started dogs varies greatly depending upon the breeder/trainer you select, most started dogs will possess basic gun dog skills. A typical started dog will have the ability to find and flush game, will have been conditioned to gun fire, is able to retrieve shot birds (although not necessarily to hand), and will have undergone basic obedience training, responding to such commands as "here", "hup" or "sit", and "heel." A good started dog should be crate trained and house broken (more or less). A rule of thumb is that a sound started dog should be capable of completing its American Kennel Club Junior Hunter title (see section on Hunt Tests) without the new owner having to invest a large amount of additional training time (other than learning how to handle your new friend).

A started dog, however, is exactly what its name implies. It has been "started" on the road toward becoming a finished gun dog, but you cannot expect a started gun dog to be highly polished. Instead, make certain you have a chance to observe the dog before you buy it. If you have bought a puppy from a breeder who will raise and "start" the dog for you, make sure you and the breeder agree up-front on

Young Locke Ridge KC JH WDX: A started dog going through its paces. (Photo by Tony Roettger).

your expectations. Most reputable breeders/trainers will want to be clear not only on your expectations, but what they will expect from you as well. It is very much a two-way street. Really good breeder/trainers will evaluate you as much as you evaluate them. The best breeder/ trainers will insist that you be thoroughly pleased with your new family member, and are prepared to back that up with a money-back guarantee. Be leery of those who do not make such an offer. After all, they have at lot a stake–their reputations–in each transaction.

If you are fortunate to find the breeder/trainer close to home, you will often find you embark upon a new friendship as well. A sound relationship with a good breeder/trainer can be extremely important for the urban gun dog owner. Often professional breeder/trainers can offer training tips, provide facilities, and additional training with birds that are completely beyond the capabilities of the typical urban gun dog owner. Should the proud new owner of a started dog elect to pursue field trials and hunt tests as an additional and extremely enjoyable side benefit to owning a gun dog, your breeder/trainer can provide invaluable assistance in understanding the finer nuances of these activities.

When you pick up your dog, plan to spend as much time as you can (more than a four-hour introductory session) with your breeder/trainer to get to know your dog. This is especially important for novice gun dog owners. Bonding with, as well as learning to handle, your dog is a key success ingredient to the acquisition of a really good, started dog. By investing your time up-front in getting to know your dog and what it takes to handle him, you will be much further down the path toward your ultimate objective–a dog highly suited for both field work, but extremely comfortable in today's urban setting.

Fernmoss Jessica, a nice started dog. (Photo by Tony Roettger).

Horror stories abound about gun dog owners who pick up a started dog and immediately place the dog, unfamiliar with the new owner or his handling techniques, in a hunting situation in which the hunter expects the dog to perform flawlessly–usually in front of hunting buddies of many years. Some of these stories are the stuff from which urban legends are made. This much is certain; however, woe be unto the person foolish enough to expect a started dog to perform well under such conditions. Without the new owner taking the time to get to know the dog, his handling characteristics, and his own limitations as a handler (especially if the new owner is a novice), the chances of success are minimal.

Finished dogs

If you have money to burn, have very specific requirements, or had

Warrener's Baird's Sandpiper MH, owner Richard Bend, a finished dog is a thing of beauty. (Photo by Chip Schleider).

11

more than your share of bird dogs, you might wish to procure a "finished dog." A finished dog means that your new friend has more than just basic gun dog training or in the parlance of the AKC, exhibits those characteristics and training roughly equivalent to that of the advanced Senior Hunter. A really good finished dog will be, in all likelihood, around two or more years old, capable of finding and flushing a range of game birds while hunting in control. He will be steady to flush and shot, capable of retrieving to hand, trained to find dead game (or to perform "hunt deads" in the lexicon of the field trial and hunt test), and a good swimmer capable of water retrieves. In short, this is a dog fully trained in the arts of the field. This is not to say that a finished dog will be perfect in all respects. Just as in started dogs, there are no real standards that describe what truly constitutes a "finished dog."

In the case of the urban dweller, the term "finished dog" has an additional meaning. A truly finished urban gun dog *will be fully capable of being a sound companion for the home as well as the field*. This means a finished urban gun dog must also be fully socialized to people and

Laborador retriever, Oak Alley Cotton Chopper (Trap) owned by Paul McGagh makes a spectacular retrieve. (Photo by Dave Williams).

other dogs, totally in control (heels extremely well, returns immediately to your command of "here," knows to avoid automobiles, and is fully house trained). House training in this context means that the dog does his business only outside not on your favorite rug or carpet. It also means that the dog is capable of "living" in your house as a member of your family without chewing your easy chair to pieces or driving your spouse up the wall by running madly around the house in search of birds. The additional obedience training required of the urban gun dog likely means that you will pay handsomely for this type of dog. It also means that those acquiring a finished dog probably need additional training as handlers–especially if they are novices.

The Strategy of Breed Selection

We feel strongly that proper breed selection in any situation, (but especially for the urban setting), can go very far toward improving your chances for successfully matching a dog to your personal situation. It will also assist you in potentially reducing your training time and increasing your probability of obtaining a really sound dog for the field, hunt test, field trial, and home.

Spaniels and retrievers vary greatly in their adaptability to urban life. You need to spend time and effort to talk to breeder/trainers and conduct research to obtain as much information on the sporting breeds. To assist you in your search for the right dog, we suggest you consider the following breed selection strategy:

English springer spaniel SR Roettger's Ridge's Dixie Chic SH delivers a Dokken™ Dead Fowl Trainer and a freshly shot pheasant. (Photos by Chip Schleider).

13

Ch. Kindred Etoile le Diamant (Molly) owned by Bobbi Kolehouse.

American cocker spaniels are making a comeback in the field. Duet Diamond Double, WD. (Photos by Bobbi Kolehouse).

English cocker spaniels Phatlands Northern Skye, MH and Outwest Willie Ketchem, SH after a hard, but productive day in the field. (Photo by Tony Roettger).

+ Carefully match breed types, to your personal situation BEFORE you make your breed choice; the level of training you want your dog to have before you buy him; and your objectives in the field.

+ Focus your search on field-bred versions of your dog that have the greatest following, the largest selection, and most breeder/trainers available.

+ Go to spaniel/retriever hunt tests that tend to attract a variety of breed types, talk to owners, and observe the dogs before making your selection.

+ Evaluate grooming needs, temperament, dog size, size of the breed's gene pool, and health history of the sire and dam.

As you begin your research into the specific breed you seek, your will find that your eye will be drawn to many types of dogs. We recommend that if your objective is a serious hunting dog or field trial dog, you should concentrate on the more widely available field-bred spaniels and retrievers. This is not to say that the less widely available or more exotic spaniel and retriever breeds do not make capable gun dogs. They can and they do. However, you will find the highest potential of obtaining a sound flushing gun dog for the urban environment from the widely available spaniel and retriever field breeds. These breeds generally have the most breeder/trainers, the largest selection of hunt test and field trial clubs, and

Boykin spaniel, HRCH UH Just Ducky's Justforkicks "Mule," hard on a retrieve owner Chris Meurett. (Photo by Pam Kadlec).

register the largest number of dogs on an annual basis.

Rare or hard to find field spaniel and retriever breeds also offer potentially solid gun dogs for town and field, but are generally much more limited in terms of breeder/trainers, clubs catering to the breed, and overall dog numbers than mainstream dogs. They also generally have a more restricted gene pool for the field strains, and gun dogs from this category are often far more difficult to find. The rarer breeds generally are primarily bench dogs that still exhibit field characteristics, and often have been away from the hunting world for several generations. Although these dogs generally may possess the charm, beauty, and disposition to be wonderful housedogs, their often-diminished field instincts may reduce significantly the chances of ultimately obtaining your goal. Unless the buyer is extremely experienced in gun dog selection and training, the typical urban gun dog buyer, especially the novice, may wish to stick to mainstream field bred dogs to increase his or her chance of success.

Due to the many superb books on gun dog breeds, we have not sought here to discuss individual breeds. Excellent general sources for gun dog breed information are Charles

A beautiful golden retriever — Goldwood Tuck of Joy "Tuck " owned by Joan and Cliff Hilton of Goldwood Kennels in White Bear Lake, Minnesota. (Photos by Joan Hilton).

CH ShawnDe's Tiddlywinks SH, WDX, CDX, MX, AXJ, a Welsh springer spaniel owned by Cheryl Clark and Randy Capsel makes a dynamic retrieve. (Photo by Randy Capsel).

A very talented young Sussex spaniel Arundel's Clementine Churchill owned by Michael Globetti makes a wonderful presentation of a goose. (Photo by Michael Globetti).

Left: A Sussex spaniel, Ch. Stonecroft Cosenza, WD, CGC, emerges from the water after making a nice retrieve of a downed chukar partridge. (Photo by Ann McGloon). Right: A Riverly Feather Chaser WD, a nice looking field spaniel, owned by Tony Belak, going through its paces. (Photo by Tony Roettger).

Fergus' *Gun Dog Breeds: A Guide to Spaniels, Retrievers, and Pointing Dogs,* and *The Encyclopedia of North American Sporting Dogs.* James B. Spencer's classic, *HUP! Training Flushing Spaniels the American Way*, now in its second edition, contains excellent summaries of the characteristics of the various spaniel breeds. It belongs on the bookshelf of every serious spaniel and retriever trainer interested in obtaining a solid flushing dog.

Health Considerations, Registration, and Picking your Dog

An essential consideration for anyone seeking to buy a flushing dog is that of the genetic health of the dog. Spaniels, retrievers, and other breeds suffer from certain genetic problems that often do not appear until after the dog is fully grown. Until the advent of modern veterinarian genetic testing techniques, it was often a crapshoot as to whether you had bought a dog that would eventually exhibit one of these debilitating and often heartbreaking ailments. Rather than take the "roll the dice" approach, it is best to narrow the odds in your favor. This is where your breeder/trainer selection is really important. But the burden is not the breeder's alone. The prospective urban gun dog owner needs to have a basic understanding of the hereditary problems facing many of the flushing and retrieving breeds prior to jumping into dog selection.

18

GENETIC OR HEREDITARY EYE DISORDERS: There are several hereditary or genetic canine eye disorders that affect spaniels and retrievers: progressive retinal atrophy (PRA) which eventually results in blindness, retinal dysplasia which is a mild deformation of the retina, and eyelid defects. The Canine Eye Registry Foundation (CERF) provides a certification that the eyes of dogs are clear of hereditary disorders at the time of examination. You should ask your breeder/trainer for a certification for the parents of your dog and request that your puppy undergo an eye examination by an American College of Veterinarian Ophthalmologists certified veterinarian. The CERF examination is not a DNA test, but a physical examination. It should be performed yearly.

CANINE HIP DYSPLASIA is probably one of the most common genetic problems facing dogs today. A good way to minimize your risk of obtaining a puppy or started dog with this problem is to request certification of normal hips of both the Dam and the Sire of your dog. The Orthopedic Foundation for Animals (OFA) is at present the most widely accepted certifying authority. Canine hip dysplasia is an abnormality of the hip joints that is usually detectable in younger dogs, around two years of age, by hip x-rays. The end result is a debilitating lameness for the dog that caused by inflammation of the joints. Recently the AKC started to put the OFA certification numbers of the Sire and Dam on puppies' AKC registration papers to provide evidence that the test was actually performed. Your breeder should also be able to provide you with the OFA number so you can do an on-line check of any dog the breeder may have as breeding stock.

Hip Dysplasia is a heartbreaking genetic condition for which there is no known cure. Your best bet for reducing the risk of obtaining an afflicted dog is by interviewing the breeder/trainer as to the medical history of the Dam and Sire of your dog and following up by requesting OFA certification.

CANINE PHOSOPHOFRUCTOKINASE (PFK): Another genetic condition the prospective buyer needs to be on the lookout for is PFK. This is a recessive genetic disease afflicting spaniels. PFK essentially affects the dog's ability to convert sugar into energy thereby creating causing the dog to fatigue rapidly. This intolerance of exercise is caused by the destruction of red blood cells creating a form of anemia in the dog. Genetic PFK testing can determine whether a dog has a recessive PFK gene. If a dog tests "normal/clear" for PFK, it indicates that the spaniel does not have the trait and can be safely, at least as far as PFK goes, bred. Dogs can be determined to be carriers of the disease with no apparent symptoms of the PFK affliction. Unfortunately, a carrier can pass the disease on to future generations. If, however, the dog tests "affected" for PFK, he or she has the disease and will be unable to withstand the rigors of the field.

Taking the time up-front to ensure that your dog is reasonably clear of hereditary disorders is a little time consuming, but extremely important step in the selection of a healthy dog. Reputable professional breeder/trainers routinely provide these certifications, usually without the buyer requesting them, but you also should take the initiative to ensure your new friend is not at risk from hereditary eye or hip disorders.

In short, with research, thought, and patience, you will find a dog that possesses the right temperament and field skills and be healthy at home in the city and in the country.

Registration, Titles, Ancestry, Common Sense and Dog Selection:

You have settled on the field breed you want; you have settled on a list of reputable breeder/trainers that have litters of puppies; you have requested and received the health information that confirms the litter is free of debilitating hereditary diseases. Your next task is to examine the ancestry of the puppies. Are they registered with one of the two major kennel clubs in the United States–the American Kennel Club or the United Kennel Club? The American Kennel Club, the largest of the two major US kennel clubs, holds the registries of the most purebred dogs in the United States as well as licensing performance and conformation events for clubs throughout the country. It awards specific titles for winning competitive field trials such as FC (Field Champion), AFC (Amateur Field Champion), CFC (Canadian Field Champion) or NFC (National Field Champion). The AKC also awards titles for each of three levels of its hunt test program, as do the United Kennel Club, the North American Hunting Retriever Association, and various spaniel and retriever breed organizations.

20

Title prefixes and suffixes can be quite confusing. Several years ago one of our acquaintances received a telephone call from a very earnest buyer seeking a field-bred English springer spaniel. During the telephone conversation, the prospective buyer raved about the family's previous dog because it had a CGC title at the end of its name. Our hapless buyer was under the mistaken impression that the older dog was a "Canine Grand Champion"–a true world champion. Our friend, did not have the heart to tell the person that a CGC is a Canine Good Citizen award given to a dog that can sit for 30 seconds without attacking judge or gallery while left unattended–unfortunately not a Canine Grand Champion. Take the time to study title suffixes and prefixes. A good source for understanding the title award system ave the AKC's NAHRA's and UKC's websites (see also Chapter 9).

An AKC or UKC registered dog from field-bred stock helps to indicate that your puppy has the potential to become a sound hunting dog. Title prefixes and suffixes to the Sire and Dam also help indicate hunting talent in the bloodlines of the parents. Talk to the breeder/ trainer; ask questions and visit the kennel to view the litter if possible. For example:

✦ Has the Dam been bred before? If so, how many times? When was her most recent breeding prior to the current litter?

✦ To whom were the puppies sold–hunting homes or companion homes? (nothing wrong with the pet homes but, if you want a hunting dog, a breeder specializing in companion dogs may not be the best choice).

✦ What titles, if any, do the Sire and Dam possess? Is there a Field Champion (FC) before the name? Are there any suffixes in the titles such as MH (Master Hunter), SH (Senior Hunter), or JH (Junior Hunter) awarded by the American Kennel Club or prefixes conferred by the United Kennel club?

✦ What is the state of their overall health? Have they had their shots and tails docked, if they are spaniels? If the tails have been docked, are they short or long docks? Field breeders generally dock their puppies' tails longer than do bench breeders.

+ Do they look healthy and playful, or are they lethargic?
+ If buying a started or finished dog, ask to see a demonstration of the dog's hunting prowess. Does the dog retrieve, tolerate gun shot noise, possess a good nose for finding game, and handle reasonably well?

If you are buying a started dog and the breeder/trainer indicates that the pups will hunt, definitely seek a demonstration of their capabilities. If it is a young puppy you are after, ask the breeder to show you something the parent can do as a hunting dog. A basic retrieve is a good start. Hunt test titles are also a good indication of hunting ability. But a word of caution here, although Hunt Test titles mean the sire and dam or started dog can hunt, bear in mind that there is a significant difference between a Junior Hunter and a Field Champion. With hunt test titles, it is also good to ask how long it took for the sire, dam, or started dog to pass the hunt test levels. For example, if it took them ten chances for a dog to obtain a Junior Hunter title that, on the surface, appears to be a few too many attempts. Shop around a little more. Similarly, parents with field championship pedigrees, such as sometimes indicated in newspaper advertisements, could mean that the great, great grandfather was a Field Champion–especially if that is the only FC in the pedigree. Finally, look at the parents. Only the female may be available for viewing but the breeder should give you the sire's owner's telephone number or email address for further investigation.

There is no real science or trick to picking a puppy from a litter. It really comes down to selecting the puppy you like most and hoping that you get the right mix of traits. No matter how well you do your homework, picking a puppy or a started dog with the "right stuff" is still a roll of the dice. However, you can substantially improve the odds by sound research, asking the right questions, and using a healthy dose of common sense.

TWO

Where, When, and How to Train in the City

A daunting challenge for the urban gun dog trainer is the question: where the heck do you go to train a dog in the city, especially if you do not own property in the country? How does one go about constructing a training regime for gun dogs without the expanses of territory routinely seen in gun dog training videos? Where *do* those guys get all that time to dedicate to gun dog training? The answer of course is that they are professionals who are themselves highly trained, well-equipped, and possessed of training sites suitable to their professional requirements. The professionals have been training and handling dogs for many years and have organized their lives around their professions. When compared to the professional trainer, the amateur urban gun dog trainer operates at a distinct disadvantage. One of the underlying assumptions of this book is that the urban flushing dog owner has *extremely limited space and time* in which to train his or her dog.

Where to Train

Finding suitable training space is often *the* major challenge to training a gun dog. For example, if you live in a townhouse or an apartment, the term "yard training" has little relevance to your personal situation. If you are fortunate enough to own a single family dwelling with a nice-sized yard, you have an advantage over the townhouse and apartment-leasing crowd. Some townhouse resident associations have deed restrictions on pet ownership. Similarly, many apartment complexes flat out refuse to lease to dog owners. Merely finding a good match between residences permitting dog ownership and your personal requirements can be tough enough, let alone finding places to train.

Prejudices against dogs in general and hunting dogs in particular often are a major fact of life in the city and serve as a significant limiting factor in finding suitable training areas. Many of us have encountered neighbors who harbor a fear or innate dislike of dogs that borders on the hysterical and are willing to call the animal control authorities the second you appear with your dog off lead. Well-intentioned neighborhood management associations that exert dictatorial control over common areas may also be an impediment. There is no denying the fact that many people living in today's urban settings have lost touch with the heritage of the field. Therefore, many people mistakenly correlate training a dog for the field or hunting with wanton destruction of wildlife, or assume that those who hunt are illiterate, gun-toting, red-necked country bumpkins with no respect for nature. It is unfortunate, but these attitudes and stereotypes tend to be held more by city dwellers than those raised in rural America–and they persist. It is a sad state of affairs that many urban inhabitants blame the decline of wildlife on hunters rather than real root causes of habitat destruction stemming from unchecked development and intensive farming techniques. Good hunters with well-trained dogs practice game conservation for ethical reasons and for preservation of the sport.

All of these obstacles and more face the urban gun dog owner in identifying suitable training areas. We have found it is better to face these stumbling blocks head-on and anticipate them in seeking training locations. *If you clearly identify your training area limitations, you can put in place a plan to overcome them.* Location is an important psychological and philosophical component of training and has a significant impact upon the frequency of training. As inhabitants of cities and as creatures of habit, we tend to follow set routines and schedules mentally calculating, either consciously or subconsciously, the distances to restaurants, entertainment facilities, and grocery stores, in terms of travel time from our home. We have found that the best way to conceptualize training areas in the urban environment is as a series of concentric circles starting within your home and radiating outward in increasing distances measured in travel time (not actual distance) from your home.

HOME: The home—we live in it, often take it for granted, and generally dismiss it as a training area. However, your home remains one of the best training locations you have at your disposal for all levels of gun dog training. It is readily available, can be configured (within reason) to your training needs, and offers a uniquely bounded, risk-reduced area to help your dog progress. *It is the primary location the city dweller initially will use for training his gun dog.* Corridors and hallways are some of the best training areas in your home. A closed corridor is an excellent place to undertake beginning "here" and retrieve training. We use a closed corridor to train puppies to come when called, to begin the process of retrieving, undertake basic training for steadying to thrown dummies, "place" training, and to do initial "heeling" training. The closed corridor provides a bounded area where your dog has no exit, except through you—in essence a "no fail zone." By eliminating choices, you create an environment where it is extremely difficult for your dog not to succeed. This in turn leads to a constant re-enforcement of the command and your dog's development of confidence in his understanding of the command—an essential ingredient in the training process. Consult Joe Arnette's and George Hickox's superb book *Hunt 'Em Up* for an excellent model of how the retrieving corridor helps create an environment for success when training your gun dog.

BASEMENTS, if you happen to have one, also provide excellent bounded areas much like closed corridors. Their principle advantage over corridors is that the area in a basement tends to be greater than that of a closed corridor. Garages can provide a suitable alternative to basements when cleaned up and devoid of vehicles, dangerous objects, and distractions. If you do not have a basement or a garage and your spouse is supportive of your indoor training regime, you may from

25

time to time be able to use your den or living room for a little training. We suggest that when forced to use the den or living room, concentrate on basic obedience training. Depending upon the personality and size of your dog, the urban trainer can also do short retrieves. Common sense dictates that the living room is not the place to engage in highly rambunctious gun dog training. Carefully assess your home and its potential for suitable training before developing your training plan. It is time well spent. In subsequent chapters on specific training techniques we start with what can be accomplished indoors, then move outside for the next level of training.

Roettger Ridge's Rivendell (Arwen), a nice young English cocker spaniel, works on retrieving in the garage. (Photo by Chip Schleider).

YARDS AND COMMON AREAS: Examine the yard next (if you live in a single-family dwelling) or available common areas if you happen to live in an apartment or townhouse. The yard is the next most important training area. An urban gun dog trainer can accomplish miracles in the yard with dedication, patience, and persistence. Take a critical look at your yard or common area. Are there small children who frequent the area or live next door? Is the property next to a major thoroughfare? What restrictions are there from neighborhood associations, management associations, or apartment managers? Are there local ordinances imposing restrictions on pets that apply to your situation, such as leash laws, pooper-scooper laws, or similar constraints? How understanding are your neighbors? Again, the goal here is to clearly understand the limitations, pitfalls, and ob-

Yards are superb for the basics. (Photo by Randy Jahnke).

stacles you potentially face when training in the immediate outdoors and develop a plan to address these issues. To ensure you do not make enemies in the neighborhood, stuff a plastic bag in your pocket when you train in common or other public areas to pick up that occasional pooper that appears when you least expect it. It helps with public relations.

PARKS, PLAYING FIELDS, AND URBAN RECREATION AREAS: A great place to train, assuming the trainer complies with the local laws concerning pets, is an out of the way area of a park, a ball field not being used, or other playgrounds and open recreation areas. These generally require a little scouting and prior planning, but can be used during non-peak hours. Many city parks are quite large and have large open areas that are lightly or seasonally used. For example, during the late fall, winter, and early spring months when the weather is relatively chilly, you might find that you have the park, playground, or ball field virtually to yourself. However, weekends and holidays are certain to be more crowded, especially in the late spring, summer, and early fall. Plan your training times accordingly. Public areas such as parks, playgrounds, and recreation areas can be perfect locations for many of the drills discussed in subsequent chapters. But, you need to use common sense and check to ensure you comply with all local laws and ordinances concerning pets and the particular area you are seeking to use for your training.

CONSERVATION SOCIETIES, SPORTING DOG CLUBS, GAME PRESERVES, AND PROFESSIONAL TRAINING FACILITIES: Excellent training areas are often available as a by-product of membership in a conservation society.

For example, the Isaac Walton League of America, one of the nation's oldest conservation groups, often has land associated with its clubs throughout the United States. Members can use this land for a variety of different pursuits–hunting, fishing, clay target shooting, and dog training. Similarly, the Nature Conservancy has invested significantly in obtaining large tracts of land to protect indigenous species and to preclude development. Some tracts are surprisingly close and within a short driving distance from urban areas. Ducks Unlimited, Pheasants Forever, Quail Unlimited, the Ruffed Grouse Society, and similar societies generally have clubs in many urban areas and may have access to land convenient to your location. They are also a good way to network with people who share your interests and have taken to heart the mission to protect America's natural resources.

FIND AND JOIN A SPORTING DOG CLUB IN YOUR VICINITY: These clubs can be quickly identified using the internet or by references from your breeder/trainer. Hunting spaniel and retriever clubs generally include all spaniel and retriever types and enthusiastically welcome you to their ranks as a lover of a flushing dog. Often hunting spaniel and retriever clubs will embrace a region and draw members from various cities and towns. If your tastes run to retrievers, you will find a large number of hunting retriever clubs catering to the outdoorsman. These clubs generally hold training days, have access to land where their members can train, and provide "group therapy," positive re-enforcement, access to birds, sponsor hunts, and provide instruction for the novice trainer. If you are at all serious about training your dog for the field, membership in a spaniel or retriever hunting club is perhaps the best way for a city dweller to gain access to training areas.

GAME PRESERVES are wonderful resource for the urban gun dog trainer. Perceived by many as the future of all upland game hunting as game birds grow increasingly scarce, game preserves offer the urban gun dog trainer distinct potential for gaining access to training areas and to birds for training. Many game preserves actually started out as gun dog training kennels, but expanded to provide bird shooting for land-starved urban hunters. An excellent source for game preserves throughout the United States is *Black's Wing and Clay*. This superb handbook is a must for wingshooters and dog trainers. It lists game

Game preserves need not be far from home. SR Roettger Ridge's Dixie Chic SH retrieves a Chukar partridge shot on a game preserve 4 miles from Dulles International Airport. (Photo by Chip Schleider).

preserves, dog training suppliers, conservation organization contact information, wingshooting destinations domestically and internationally, shotgun supplies, and shotgun manufacturers. Updated and published annually, it is a single, comprehensive source for almost all of your shotgunning needs.

PROFESSIONAL DOG TRAINING FACILITIES If you are extremely fortunate to live within reasonable driving distance of one, operated by a well-respected breeder/trainer of flushing dogs this is perhaps the best location for dog training. For example, at Roettger Ridge Kennels in North Branch, Minnesota, each weekend finds ten to fifteen dog owners predominately from the twin cities area training their spaniels. As do other professional training facilities, Roettger Ridge provides birds, training for dogs and handlers, gunners, comprehensive gun dog training, and boarding. Similar facilities operated by professional breeder/trainers exist in various locations throughout the nation. You may have hit the jackpot and found a breeder/trainer conveniently located near your city of residence. If, like one of the authors, you happened to buy your dog from a breeder/trainer living a thousand miles away, you can still draw upon the expert knowledge of breeder/trainer in seeking to locate a professional near your home. Professional hunting spaniel and retriever breeders and trainers comprise a relatively small community. Through field trials, hunt test participation, sire and dam selection for breeding, conferences, and judging field events, professional breeder/trainers develop networks that span the nation. If you have done your homework properly and selected a breeder/trainer whose standards, quality of breeding and training, and reputation are second to none, you can count on their recommendations for professionals close to you with whom you can train.

WILDLIFE MANAGEMENT AREAS, STATE PARKS AND FORESTS, NATIONAL PARKS, AND PUBLIC LANDS: Almost every state in the Union has set aside wildlife management areas and state forests for the preservation of habitat for multiple wildlife species. In many states these management areas are open to hunting and the training of gun dogs. These areas provide a superb environment in which to train a young flusher in basic gun dog skills. In addition to identifying those wildlife management areas close to home, carefully review the applicable game regulations and licensing requirements for training gun dogs in these areas. Some states limit the training of gun dogs on state lands and even require a type of license for gun dog training. Although pigeons (rock dove) are not a licensed game bird in any state we know, there may be constraints on their use in wildlife management areas and state forests for gun dog training. Many states also limit the training of gun dogs on game that is not in season, so be certain to research this for the state in which you reside prior to undertaking any type of gun dog training on state lands. Most states maintain web sites for their game and fish departments, which clearly outline legal constraints on training dogs on wildlife. If you cannot find information addressing gun dog training, call the department directly. It is important you clearly understand the applicable laws governing gun dog training in your state. Many a well-intentioned trainer has suffered fines or confiscated firearms for not doing research on this point.

The country's extensive national park and forest system provides additional areas for the urban trainer. Again, ensure you comply with any legal constraints and obtain the appropriate licenses. A good tip is to contact the forest rangers to obtain first hand any information on training areas or limits to gun dog training. Generally speaking, national forests are open to hunting, whereas national parks may or may not be open to hunting and gun dog training. Do your homework, and you may find that a conveniently located national forest or park could be just the area you need to polish those flushing dog skills.

When and How to Train

If your life is anything like the lives of the authors, driving home after a long day of work in bumper-to-bumper traffic only to pick up your dog, turn around and drive out again for an hour or so before getting in a half hour of training before dark, and then driving home does not sound particularly inviting. It actually sounds downright masochistic. More reasonable people would head directly to the refrigerator, withdraw a suitably chilled bottle of their favorite beer, pop the cap, take off their shoes and settle into their most comfortable easy chair, and watch the nightly news. The last thing on any sane person's mind after a hard day at work would be working with a young dog that is jumping up on your legs, whining at the door, and staring at you with eyes that seem to say, "Get your butt out of that chair and come play with me."

Although there are times guilt is a strong motivator, it has been our experience urban gun dog trainers operate most effectively when they have a training plan tied to specific training objectives that, in turn, take into consideration the urban environment as well as the capabilities of both the dog and the trainer. Only a good training plan will help the urban gun dog trainer to balance the myriad of interests competing for the dog owner's time in today's fast paced urban setting. This book is, in essence, a detailed training plan. However, you will have to customize it by making the lessons of this book relevant to your personal situation.

The key to a good plan is to *evaluate the amount of time* you have to dedicate to your canine friend. Plan to dedicate at least thirty minutes daily to training–do not plan for two days of two-hour sessions during the weekend with no training during the week. Consistent, frequent, and relative short periods of training will enable your dog to make significant strides. Plan also to incorporate little five-minute training sessions such as having your dog sit for increasingly longer periods of time, or place training during your normal home routine.

Clearly *assess your objectives* in gun dog training that you seek for you and your dog on a daily, weekly, and monthly basis and develop a training plan that meets your requirements. Do you want a solid hunting companion and care little for the field trial or hunt test scene? Are you seeking to put ribbons on the wall from the head-to-head competition that typifies field trials? Is your objective to measure you and your dog against the increasingly demanding standards of the hunt test to gain coveted titles? If hunting is your goal, what type of hunting do you do? Are you primarily an upland game hunter seeking grouse, quail, or pheasant? Do you hunt waterfowl most frequently, but also shoot the occasional pheasant? Are you mostly a dove hunter?

Each one of the goals implied by the preceding questions demands a slightly different training approach. Spaniels and retrievers are more than capable of performing the tasks these goals demand, but they must have tailored training plans to be able to do so. For example, if you are mostly a dove, duck, and goose hunter with quail on that special trip to Georgia or the annual pilgrimage to the mid-west for pheasants, you may wish to concentrate heavily on what is called non-slip retriever training. Non-slip retriever training emphasizes a steady dog at your side that is sent for marked and unmarked retrieves as you shoot the dove, duck, or goose. Both breed types can perform non-slip retriever work well, but their training must incorporate the tasks they will be expected to perform in the field. They also should incorporate a good regime of training in finding, flushing, and retrieving shot birds, as they would be expected to do in the flatlands of the mid-western pheasant states.

On the other hand, if your objective is field trials and hunt tests, you will concentrate more on quartering in braces, steadiness to wing and shot, hunt dead scenarios, blind retrieves, and water work consistent with the standards of either the field trial or the hunt test. Your training regime for your gun dog in this instance will emphasize hunting form, aggressive bird finding, controllability, and the ability to take handling directions. In short, you must understand exactly what tasks your finished gun dog should primarily be asked to accomplish and tailor your training plan accordingly.

In developing your plan, however, also consider the following: if this is your first gun dog (all of us have had to start somewhere), your plan will have to include *training for you as well as your dog*. You will have to clearly analyze your capabilities and lack thereof to develop a plan that meets both of your needs. One also must recognize that dogs, like people, learn at different rates. Because each dog is unique, a pro forma or cookie cutter plan that adheres to a rigid time schedule will be more frustrating than the absence of a plan altogether. At each training milestone, you must be totally convinced your dog has thoroughly mastered the objectives you have set for your dog prior to moving on to the next level. Common sense also dictates each phase of your plan be periodically adjusted to ensure your schedule corresponds to your dog's capabilities. Make sure to incorporate periodic reviews peppered with a little time off for you both.

The philosophy of dog training, especially in the spaniel breeds, is something to which one needs to give some serious thought. Dogs in general respond more to positive than negative re-enforcement, and flushing dogs are no exception. Flushing dogs, especially spaniels are intelligent and generally mild-tempered dogs. A soft hand in training spaniels (retrievers as well) is probably a good starting point, especially for the novice trainer. Some important principles apply to training:

- Patience
- Consistency
- Repetition
- Re-enforcement
- Moderation
- Tailored Training
- Knowing when to quit

Patience is the *sine qua non* of dog training; the exercise of patience implies an even-tempered approach to training your dog. All of us have fixed in our minds the individual who has completely lost self-control seeking to heel an unresponsive dog–red-faced, handling the dog roughly, intimidating, loud, and angry. He repeats his command. "Heel!" The dog looks at the trainer with questioning eyes, uncertain as to what specifically he has done wrong, and fails to perform to the trainer's expectation. The trainer increasingly reddens, yells, and yanks harder at the lead–the dog straining wildly to get away.

In this scenario, nothing positive is accomplished and a good deal of harm may have been done. A prime rule for the trainer *is to cease training if you are about to lose your patience*. Patience is multifaceted as it requires the trainer to be even tempered with the dog, to control himself or herself, or to be prepared to take a step backward and repeat a previously learned lesson.

Consistency allows a dog to learn a lesson the same way every time. It accelerates the dog's ability to learn as it eliminates extraneous variables. Giving the same command the same way each time is only part of consistency. Give a command only once; if your dog fails to comply, do not give the command again, but physically (not roughly) ensure that your dog complies with the command. For example, you give the command to "hup" and your faithful friend fails to comply, do not give the command continually, but physically place your dog in the sitting position. This type of consistency will teach your dog that you mean business the first time and every time you give the command.

Dogs learn through repetition and association. The more a dog repeats a command, the more entrenched it becomes. Repetition is the handmaiden of patience. It takes a heck of a lot of patience to give a command over and over and over again. But believe us, the more you repeat it, the more deeply your dog will learn it.

The first rule of wing walking is you never let go one wing strut before having a solid hold on the next wing strut. It is the same with dog training; the trainer must make certain that he or she has a sound hold on the basic commands before moving to the next level. Lenin probably put it the best when describing the progress of modernization during the Russian revolution as "one step forward, two steps back." Re-enforcement of your commands means from time to time you will have to devote attention to review, especially if you perceive your dog seems to be backsliding. Spend some time on review; it will help you and the dog move to the next level.

Training is best done in moderation. Many small lessons spanning minutes are better than one single two-hour block. Training in moderation means that both you and the dog are fresh for each session, and quit on a positive note. Dogs have a relatively short attention span, and will lose interest over time. Plan your lessons to be short with rest between them. If you tend to have a short fuse, a short lesson will help you with patience as well.

Just as in raising children, there is no rigid timeline to training dogs. Dogs, like humans, learn at different rates. Those of us with children know this lesson very well. We worry our child is not progressing at the same rate (read timeline) as someone else's child. Tutors are employed, playtime is curtailed, homework is checked, re-checked, and then checked again. In short, in the highly competitive world of cities, we drive our children mercilessly to excel. The result is highly predictable–stressed out parents, burned out children, harried teachers, and a whole host of psychological problems to unravel as everyone ages. Folks, we are here to tell you that if you take this approach to dogs you are doomed to failure. Both of us have witnessed time and again the results of highly competitive dog training in the field trial circuit. Dogs are like kids in this respect. Each dog progresses at his or her own rate; therefore, each dog will move on to the next level at a different rate. Those who train dogs for a living know this well. Do not be duped by those who tell you a dog needs to be at certain level by a certain age. Learn to read your dog. The great dog trainer, Richard Wolters, outlined the progress of a dog he was training in terms of a timeline. Many novices and quite a few experienced trainers believe at a certain age, a dog must have mastered very specific tasks. We, on the other hand, advocate the maturity line. Simply stated, forget about time when training a dog. When the dog has fully mastered a lesson, move to the next level. If you follow this approach, you concentrate on reading your dog. In the end, you will learn as much about yourself as you do the dog. Who knows, perhaps our children will benefit as well.

Finally, know when to quit. When you are accomplishing very little or your dog seems to have its head elsewhere, stop the lesson. You will learn to read your dog and yourself. When either of you reaches the saturation point, stop training and pick it up later. You will both be the better for it.

THREE

Essential Equipment for the Urban Trainer

I f you are firm subscriber to the maxim, "The one who dies with the most toys wins," then this chapter is probably not for you. There is a veritable cornucopia of gun dog goodies available through mail order catalogs and online stores. Bird launchers, tethers, electronic collars, hand-braided leather lanyards. If you are not careful you will end up with a box per week arriving on your doorstep. Many of these offerings are essential; just as many can be safely passed up without depriving you or your dog of the necessary tools needed for training. Before obtaining all mail order and online catalogs and spending hours pouring over the latest in gun dog training trinkets, think about what *you need* to get started. We summarize in this chapter those things you will really need to get started, and subsequent chapters will detail the use of this equipment.

If you are seeking to train your dog in the city, you need less equipment than you think. We will focus here on the essentials the trainer needs to get started in an urban environment. As training progresses, additional equipment will be needed, especially as you move from the immediate vicinity of your home to training areas close to the city.

PUPPY TOYS: Go to your local super retail store, pet chain, or grocery store and you will be totally overwhelmed with the all the dog toys on the market today. Most of these puppy toys, unfortunately, are of the squeaky toy variety. The main problem with squeaky toys, aside from driving a dog owner nearly insane, is that squeaky toys reward a puppy for biting down hard on an object. This, we have found, leads to the development of a hard mouth while retrieving and often a lot of mouthing of birds and retrieving dummies or bumpers. Instead of a squeaky toy, buy small hard rubber toys, such as the Kong series. Kong toys come in a variety of sizes, shapes, and models and are widely available in both grocery and large retail stores. In addition to the Kong series, tennis balls, small puppy-size bumpers, and rawhide chewies are also excellent sources of entertainment for puppies.

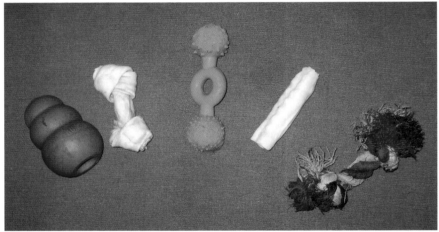

Suitable toys for puppies -- not a squeaky toy in the crowd. (Photo by Tony Roettger).

COLLARS, IDENTIFICATION PLATES, TATTOOS, AND SUBCUTANEOUS CHIPS: A collar for those residing in the city is an essential piece of equipment. Collars serve as a means to display licenses and identification in addition to serving as a means by which the trainer can affix a leash or checkcord. Gun dog owners have many collar choices; however, we recommend that you buy a broad, flat nylon or leather collar for your dog with a D-ring for attaching a lead and licenses. A broad, flat collar is better than a narrow nylon or rolled leather collar, because it does not cut into to your dog's neck to the extent that the narrow ones do.

These do not have to be expensive, but check for quality when buying the collar. There are many on the market that do not hold up in wet weather or under tough field conditions. If you elect to get a collar that enables you to affix a name plate, make sure you put your telephone number and the word "reward" on the collar, but not the dog's name in the event that you lose your dog. The dog's name is key to controlling the dog and winning his affection. Safeguard this information by not putting the dog's name on his collar.

Some breeders and veterinarians offer tattooing services to indicate ownership. You might consider this service to ensure that you will be able to readily identify your dog should you and the dog become separated and to discourage dognappers. Recently, however, a new technology has hit the market that enables your veterinarian to implant a small microchip just under the skin of your dog. This chip is connected to a national database that can be accessed by any veterinarian or animal control center. The vet uses a hand-held bar code reader-like device to scan your dog and to retrieve important ownership information. It is low cost, easily done, and virtually painless procedure that all dog owners should consider.

CHECKCORDS: The checkcord is the lifeline of the urban trainer and an essential tool throughout the training of your dog. In rural training regimes, the checkcord is used relatively sparingly or sometimes not at all. In the city, however, you'll use your checkcord more and longer than you ever will in the country during outdoor training sessions. Why is that? If a dog fails to respond to commands such as "here" or "gone away," which is used to call a dog off the chase of a flying or running bird while training in the country, the most damage the trainer generally will suffer in a rural setting is the increased heart rate, heavy breathing, and rubbery legs associated with chasing down an errant dog. Given the diversity of dangers to a dog or owner present in the city, the outcome could be far, far worse. Without a checkcord, the dog could run into the street creating a dangerous situation for the dog, the trainer, or a third party. It also could run wild through a neighbor's yard, park area, or playground causing untold social problems for its owner.

In short, training in the city requires the trainer to have the dog *totally* under control at all times. And the checkcord is the primary method to ensure your dog is under control until such time as you are *absolutely certain* that he will not run away or will come without hesitation when you call. It will be used to make that critical transition from indoor training to outdoor training.

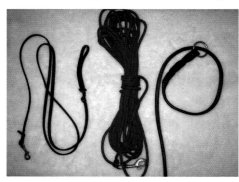

We recommend that you get a high-quality checkcord with a rounded body–not the flat kind. The rounded type of checkcord is easier to grasp firmly and gentler on your hand than the flat cord version. The cord should be round, possess a diameter of at least 7/16 inches, be approximately thirty feet long and have a snap hook for attaching to your dog's collar. The higher the quality the better, given the

A good selection of leashes, slip leads, and check cords. (Photo by Tony Roettger).

use to which it will be put. Look for those that do not tangle easily, and they will improve your quality of life.

WHISTLES: Examine a gun dog supply catalog, and you likely will see many, many different whistle types. They range from extremely loud whistles designed to call retrievers back from the afterlife, to dainty little silent whistles for enticing a Pekinese back from your bathroom. There are big whistles with peas or plastic balls inside that trill, beautiful, hand-carved staghorn whistles that have a pitch that varies from whistle to whistle, hard fixed-pitch plastic whistles that function on blown air, and all come in a variety of colors, shapes, and sizes. Choose your whistle with care. We do not recommend the extremely loud whistles used by some retriever trainers. The reason is simple. Use of an extremely loud whistle in an urban area, if done with reckless abandon, may have the unwanted consequence of summoning the local police under the mistaken impression that one is in personal danger. It just as easily could result in those law enforcement personnel knocking on your front door at the behest of an angry neighbor.

Indoor training with an extremely loud whistle will no doubt peak the ire of your family. Here, as elsewhere in this book, we call for a little common sense.

The main thing is once you start with one type of whistle, be consistent and stick with it. We recommend for spaniels an ACME 210½ or 211½ pitch black, plastic, pealess whistle secured by an inexpensive (in Tony's case a very expensive), adjustable lanyard. The entire whistle and lanyard rig can be had for under $15.00 to over $100.00, depending upon how elaborate the lanyard. They are readily available through mail order and online suppliers.

A wide variety of whistles. (Photo by Tony Roettger).

Buy two or three with low cost lanyards. We have found whistles have a tendency to spontaneously grow legs and wander off, especially just prior to the outset of a hunt, field trial, or hunt test; spares are essential.

BUMPERS AND BIRD DUMMIES: Living in the city will more than likely limit the trainer's ability to keep live birds for dog training. We recognize nothing trains a bird dog like birds. Nevertheless, a good trainer can accomplish quite a lot using bumpers and bird dummies at all stages of a gun dog's training. Urban trainers will have to carefully plan for birds and likely will not be able to train with live birds routinely. It is imperative, therefore, that at an early age, a gun dog be introduced to bumpers as well as birds and bird wings.

Dogs, like dog trainers, can be picky about bumpers, and there are more bumper and dummy styles to choose from than one can imagine. For the urban trainer, however, it really boils down to a selection of two styles of bumpers and the acquisition of several bird-mimicking types of dummies. Two sizes and styles of bumpers will do nicely for your dog depending upon age, maturity, and interest level. For puppies, seek to find 2x9 inch canvas-covered foam bumpers. These are excellent bumpers for puppies and young dogs because they are small, relatively soft, and easy for the youngster to retrieve. They are also wonderful bumpers to use during beginning indoor retrieving drills. Because these bumpers are relatively soft, they will not mark or dent walls, injure furniture, or make loud noises. They are also relatively inexpensive. Buy four to six–half in white, the other half in blaze orange. Unlike humans, dogs do not readily see blaze orange bumpers. It is important to use blaze orange when training to get your dog to use its nose rather than relying on sight to find a thrown dummy. Many retriever drills start off with white dummies, easier for the dog to see, then progress to the use of blaze orange ones.

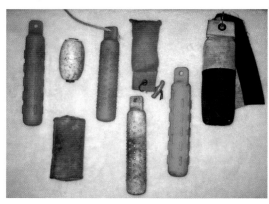

A well-worn selection of bumpers. (Photo by Tony Roettger).

For older dogs and outdoors training, we recommend that you buy about ten of the injection molded-style 2x11 inch bumpers–again one-half should be in white and the other half in blaze orange. The solid injection molded retrieving bumper, we believe, is much better (and cheaper) than the hollow rubber dummies with air valves. The hollow bumpers tend to be less durable and we have found that dogs tend to chew the bumper and the air valves. The solid injection-molded variety floats extremely well, discourages chewing and hard mouth, and throws much farther than the hollow rubber dummy. They are available through mail order and online catalogs.

One of the best products the urban trainer can invest in is the Dokken™ dead fowl dummy series. Invented by noted retriever trainer, Tom Dokken of Minnesota, these dummies are injection-molded, heavy-duty urethane with a free-swinging tough plastic head, a throwing cord, and plastic feet. These dummies throw very well, float, and mimic the general size and shape of game birds. The free-swinging head discourages playing with the bird, as it will give a dog a sharp rap on the head if your dog swings the dummy from side to side. They come in virtually all game bird varieties–both upland game and waterfowl, and can even be injected with bird scent to further enhance training. If you are training spaniels, we suggest that you pick up the quail, grouse, and one of the duck trainers. The duck trainers have the same body size as the pheasant trainer minus the hard plastic pheasant tail. The pheasant tail tends to get in the way when you throw the dummy and tangles in the dog's legs on the retrieve. The Dokken™ dead fowl trainer is an essential part of any urban training program and can be used in the basement or garage area, as well as outdoors. They are available in some sporting retail stores that cater to hunters, as well as widely available through mail order and online catalogs.

Dead Fowl Trainers™, an urban trainers best friend. (Photo by Chip Schleider).

PHEASANT, QUAIL, AND CHUKAR WINGS: One of the nicest new additions to the market is the increasing availability of bird wings as a training tool. Long used by professional trainers to engender a strong game retrieving drive early in a puppy's life, they have only recently become available through mail order and online gun dog suppliers to the general public. Next to real birds, there is nothing better than a game bird wing to get those bird dog juices flowing. We have used them, not only with puppies, but with older dogs as well. One of our best techniques is to take one of the smaller 2x9 inch canvas dummies, and affix a couple of wings to the dummy using rubber bands to simulate a shot bird. It has proven extremely effective in encouraging a young dog to retrieve dummies outdoors. For those who hunt–save, clean, and dry your bird wings. They make excellent additions to your out of doors training regime–but for the peace of the household, make sure you only use them outside.

Wings are an excellent way to get young dogs ready for birds. (Photos by Tony Roettger).

TWO SMALL BLOCKS OF WOOD CONNECTED WITH A NYLON STRING: The experienced dog trainer reading this book will certainly ask himself or herself the question, "what the heck are these for?" In the city, although he may wish otherwise, a trainer is not going to discharge his shotgun in the backyard as part of the process to condition a dog to gunfire. Similarly, in today's gun sensitive urban environment, to fire a blank pistol, as one would do in the country to mimic a shotgun blast (at a fraction of the cost of a shotgun shell), is to court disaster. How then does one begin to condition a gun dog to the sharp sound of a shotgun blast without the gun or a blank pistol? A technique we recommend is to smack together two blocks of wood. It creates a sharp sound without the use of pyrotechnics or gunpowder–and it is a darn sight cheaper. We will detail this approach in subsequent chapters–hopefully without the stifled chuckles.

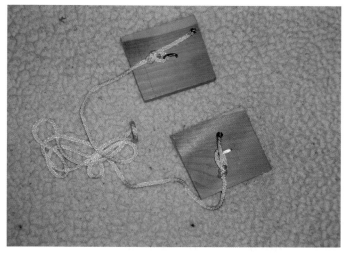

Simple wooden blocks can simulate a gunshot. (Photo by Chip Schleider).

A CHILD'S CAP GUN: This inexpensive and often overlooked tool can be purchased at almost any toy or department store. They are almost as loud as a blank pistol, but lack the "real" gun look. They can be used in your back yard without fear of having your neighbors summon your local law enforcement personnel. With due consideration for the people who live near you, a cap pistol may be used for dog training in your yard or common areas.

TRAFFIC CONES: Available in the soccer section of any large sporting goods store, these orange traffic cones are used in the more advanced stages of retriever training. They are usually available in a pack of six cones in blaze orange for less than ten dollars. These cones will be used to help your dog learn how to accomplish blind retrieves at long distances through learning how to take a "line" to the area of the fall

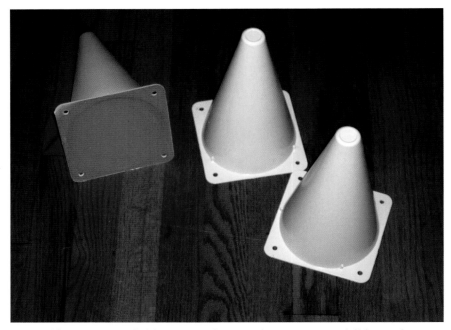

Traffic cones, available at sporting goods stores, are visible to dogs when painted white. (Photo by Chip Schleider).

of the bird or dummy. It is an essential piece of equipment for both land and water blind training.

BLANK GUNS: There comes a time in the training of every bird dog when the wood block preliminary approach to simulated gun fire needs a little more realism. Blank guns provide that bridge from wooden blocks clapped together in neighborhood training areas to superb field training. Recall the discussion on training areas, in which you will move to the training areas outside of the immediate boundaries of the city as your dog matures and develops gun dog skills. It is here the blank or primer pistol comes into play. As in almost every other area of gun dog supplies, there are a large number of choices in the blank pistol category. Most blank pistols fire .22 caliber blank cartridges, and the cost of blanks can mount quite quickly. The best choice, we believe, is one the primer pistols that use 209 shotshell primers in lieu of the more expensive blanks. One thousand primers, readily available where shotgun reloading supplies are procured–more than enough for many, many training sessions–can be procured for a fraction of the cost of .22 caliber blank cartridges. Primer pistols generally are no more expensive than blank pistols. The reduced life cycle cost associated with cheaper ammunition coupled with more widespread availability of 209 primers more than offsets any slight premium paid for a primer pistol. These are also available from gun dog supply catalogs and online stores, and can be readily shipped without special handling provisions.

DUMMY LAUNCHERS: One of the niftiest things available is the dummy launcher that combines the simulated gunfire training of the blank pistol with very long retrieves. It is one of the sexiest gun dog toys on the market today. Anyone who has ever sent a dog on a 70 plus yard water or field retrieve can tell you that the key to success is the ability of the dog to adequately mark a retrieve, take a "line" (be able to stay on a specific azimuth as indicated by the handler or the mark of a fallen bird or dummy), make the retrieve, and return with the dummy. The late, highly respected spaniel and retriever trainer, Ken Roebuck, was a firm believer in dummy launchers as a training aid. He devoted much attention to the subject of dummy launchers in his videos and book, *Gun Dog Training: Spaniels and Retrievers*. They use the propulsive power of a .22 caliber blank cartridge to launch a special dummy much farther than can be thrown by hand. Obviously, they can only be fired where you would be able to fire a blank or primer pistol, and they require a fairly large open area. Used correctly, they can be a terrific addition to a training regime by adding variety and fun; used incorrectly and they can be a danger to you and your dog. Carefully read the operating instructions and practice a few times without the added distraction of your dog in relative short grass (so you can find the darn thing after you launch it). In addition, these things kick more than a little bit, so start with the lightest load possible to get used to the launcher, and save your hand a little wear and tear.

CANINE FIRST AID KIT: A really good canine first aid kit is a great thing to put in the shopping cart when perusing an online gun dog catalog. One can only hope never to have to use it, but rest assured, somewhere along the line anyone who hunts with or trains gun dogs

Picture of dummy launcher and primer pistol. (Photo by Chip Schleider).

will have to use one or more of the items in the kit at some point. They generally come in several sizes; some kits are far more elaborate than others. The basic philosophy to which we adhere is that the best ones can be slipped into a hunting vest or coat pocket, because the larger they are, the less likely you will have it with you when you really, really need it. We will not attempt to address the subject of gun dog field first aid in this book–neither of us is a veterinarian. We will, however, recommend a couple of books on the subject that will help the gun dog owner cope with an emergency should it arise. *First Aid for Sporting Dogs*, by Charles DeVinne, DVM and *Dog First Aid: Emergency Care for the Outdoor Dog*, by Randy Acker are two short, excellent works on the subject. Both are good books, but as with any book on the subject, neither will do you a bit of good in the field unless you have thoroughly studied them in advance and practiced with your dog.

THE ESSENTIAL DOG TRAINING BAG: Once you buy all this nifty stuff, it is nice to have something to carry and store it in. The bag does not have to be fancy, but should be sufficiently large to hold your dummies and Dokken™ trainers, spare whistles, and other gun dog paraphernalia. Many gun dog suppliers offer gun dog training bags complete with whistles, dummies, and other accoutrements. We know what you're thinking at this point: "Why not buy it all at once and not have to fool around with separate purchases." The all-in-one approach is tempting to be certain, but one should not give in to the impulse. Most "complete" gun dog bags do not have all the items you want , but have many things you are not interested in acquiring. The best advice we can give is to buy the bag empty and stuff it with goodies that you select. An ideal bag will have several exterior pockets, good internal sections, and a good shoulder strap in addition to the carrying handles. Cabela's, L.L. Bean, Boyt, and other manufacturers make bags specially designed for gun dog training supplies.

PET CONTAINMENT SYSTEMS: All right, suburbanites, it is time for us to squarely address the pros and cons of today's yard pet containment systems commonly known as invisible dog fences. As far as we can tell, there is an absence of literature in gun dog books and periodicals devoted to the subject. For those blessed (or cursed depending upon one's perspective) with a nice-sized suburban yard, the thought of procuring an invisible fence is very tempting and potentially an easy way to deal with the routine of dog toilet chores.

Invisible fences operate on essentially the same principle as the electronic gun dog training collar. A small cable is buried around the circumference of the yard that emits an electronic signal. The dog is fitted with a special collar that emits a warning as the dog approaches the buried cable. The closer the dog comes to the cable the more pronounced the warning. Should the dog cross over the cable, the collar delivers a strong electronic shock to the dog. Invisible fence conditioning usually requires several of these "hair curlers" for a dog to learn that it is less than a good idea to cross the line. The dog soon learns to correlate the warning sound with both the imminence of a jolt and the geographic configuration of the buried cable. Once this process is complete, the dog is thoroughly trained and will not cross the line for fear of an electronic reprisal. Ultimately, the electronic collar is removed only once the dog understands completely its boundaries and the owner is convinced the dog will not escape. It is a truly neat invention for the dog owner who balks at the procurement of an actual fence due to esthetics or economics–especially if one detests the thought of constantly supervising the dog when let out to do its business.

Should a gun dog owner invest in one of these modern miracles? One school of thought is that the invisible fence, especially when used in a relatively small yard or to confine a small area of a more substantial area, could cause a gun dog to become "sticky" which in the lexicon of dog trainers means that the dog will not range sufficiently far from the hunter when in the field. The theory here is that the dog will hunt too close to the hunter and not cover the field sufficiently to find, flush, and retrieve game. The other school holds that today's field-bred flushing dog (no dumb bunny) will know the difference between home and field and naturally adjust quickly to life outside the invisible fence. The fence, after all, is merely an extension of the boundaries of the house. Flushing dogs, after all, hunt in close proximity to the hunter in any case, "So what's the big deal?"

Both schools are right. We believe that an invisible fence, when it covers a fairly significant area of the yard, can be used to help corral your dog. However, the trainer must build into the training plan drills designed to ensure the gun dog does not equate the fenced in area to a normal field surrounding. In order to do this, the trainer must take the dog out of the area covered by the invisible fence frequently starting at a very early age, and train in open areas as much as possible. If you elect to procure one of these fences, make certain you plan your training accordingly to ensure your dog associates the invisible fence with the house and not the field. If you do procure an invisible fence and train your dog in your backyard, be careful not to throw a dummy or bird wing close to the fence line. Your dog may shy away from the retrieve, or receive a nice little jolt for his efforts. One or two zaps from the collar, and your dog likely will develop some significant retrieving issues or cease retrieving altogether.

A Word on Electronic Collars: Perhaps the most high technology invention, as well as the most costly training aid you can buy, is the electronic collar. The best of these have a range of settings from a very low to a very high stimulus. The use of the electronic collar in dog training started with pointing dogs, because the difficulty of controlling dogs during training due to the extreme ranges these dogs cover, but spread quickly to the ranks of retriever trainers given the temperament of some hard-headed retrievers.

Professional trainers are all over the map on the issue of using electronic collars for training. Many trainers believe that the electronic collar can be used effectively to iron out the kinks in some spaniels and retrievers. For example, eCollars can be used to help steady a dog to wing and shot by keeping the dog from chasing the bird after it is flushed. Although we readily agree that the electronic collar has its uses in flushing dog training, it often creates more problems than it solves. An example of this is the early and poor application of the electronic collar in the steadying process, which has been credited with creating either "blinking," or the avoidance of birds, or the soft flush, where the dog creeps up on the bird slowly. It has also created pointing dogs out of flushing dogs.

Although many hard core retriever trainers may disagree, the use of the electronic collar in training flushing dogs for the field is extremely delicate and probably best left to professional gun dog trainers. The urban gun dog trainer, in our estimate, has little use for the electronic collars. We highly recommend that you forego them in a city setting when training flushing dogs, and suggest right up front that you seek a professional's advice on this aspect of gun dog training (see the chapter on getting professional help). This also will save you the outlay of some big bucks for a good electronic collar.

Field bred American cocker spaniel, Palmer's Rowdy Ranger SH makes a superb retrieve of a Canadian Goose. (Photo by Rich Palmer).

FOUR

Obedience Begins in the Home

A PHILOSOPHY OF GUN DOG OBEDIENCE: Obedience forms such a critical element in the development of the urban gun dog, we feel we should start with it. We have found "obedience" as applied to field dog training is a term that often appears be taken out of context. Many dog trainers and owners believe that the only "real" obedience is the dog that walks at heel, touching your leg and staring at you the entire time. No doubt it will come as a shock for many of these perfectionists to learn dogs are not automatons blindly obeying at all times. By the same token, it should not take multiple repetitions of a command, screaming, shouting, purple-turning, vein popping, foot stomping, or ranting and raving for your dog to obey.

Obedience in the city, however, is something not to be taken lightly as it is extremely important for the safety of the dog and others that a dog obeys your commands consistently and responsively. Our concept of obedience is simply a dog responds to what you, as the handler, says. Unlike dogs raised in a more rural environment, a dog raised in an urban setting will face situations that could be life threatening. For example, a dog running out of control and not responding to a call to return to its master could be struck fatally by a fast moving vehicle, or could cause an accident–unfortunate common occurrences in today's urban traffic flows.

It is, therefore, imperative for the health of all concerned, but especially for the owner's peace of mind, that obedience forms the cornerstone of urban gun dog training. Luckily for the city dweller, obedience training can be accomplished very effectively in your home. It is precisely this venue that is perhaps the most ideal place to begin basic obedience training. Initially the home offers, comparatively speaking, fewer distractions to the field-bred flushing dogs than the outdoors. The lack of animal distractions–the birds and the smells–allows you and the dog to focus on the lesson at hand. You will, however, need a relatively quiet place in which to begin. Because obedience for gun dogs is not all that different from house dogs, you may also wish to attend a basic obedience class with your dog, if you are a first time dog owner. These classes are usually fairly widely available in a city. If your town is sufficiently large enough to have one of the stores associated with a large, national pet retail chain, you often will be able to find group obedience classes there.

There are two major stages to ensuring that your puppy has learned its lesson and is ready to move on. In the first stage, you have to demonstrate to the dog what you mean by a command through repetition of the command and physically placing the dog in the position the command requires. If the command is to get off the sofa, for example, give the command "off" repeated several times while you physically move the dog off of the couch. When the dog is on the floor, you reward him with praise and a treat of choice.

We have found treats work extremely well in conditioning your puppy. Small pieces of a hotdog no bigger than your smallest fingernail, by all accounts, appear to work perhaps better than anything. Many trainers use anything from small pieces of kibble to reward a puppy to expensive dog bones or treats that have bacon, cheese, beef, and other flavors. Some even use Cheez Whiz sprayed directly into the puppy's mouth as a reward. We think this sounds a little bacchanalian and maybe is not all that good for a puppy's digestive track; try the hot dog pieces and kibble first and save the Cheez Whiz, liberally sprayed on top of crackers accompanied by a good beer for yourself after the lesson is over.

Consistent re-enforcement of the command during the first stage is key to success. Use the same command, say it firmly, but do not plead with your dog. With few exceptions, dogs do not think in complete sentences. The shorter the command, the better. Make certain everyone in the family knows the list of commands and uses the same ones. A family member of one of the authors (not to be identified), is besotted with his male boxer and consistently uses the phrase "oh Maxie baby, please be a big boy and come to papa." Unfortunately, this approach, although humorous in the extreme, does not work. In this first stage, or "show pup" stage as Joe Arnette and George Hickox refer to it, concentrate on a few essential commands in your list and work those heavily.

Once you feel as if you have made significant progress on a command, shift into the second stage. When you get there depends upon the amount of practice you have had with the dog. In stage two, you say the command only once; if your puppy does not respond to the command, place him in the proper position and reward him with praise and treat. Let's take a look at the couch example in phase two. Your dog is on the couch and you say "off" only once; he does not respond; so you physically move him off the couch. When he is off, lavishly praise him and treat him, but you never say the command more than once. If you get into the habit of saying commands repeatedly in stage two, when you move to the field, your dog will probably not listen to you until you shout a command several times, stamp your feet, and turn red-faced. The trainer must have the dog conditioned to respond first time and every time to a command.

Recall our discussion of the principles of gun dog training: consistency of commands is essential. If everyone in the household uses a different command, the problems of instilling basic obedience is exponentially increased. Call a family meeting (if you are blessed with a family) and lay out the ground rules for use of commands with the puppy. Use this opportunity to review what commands you will concentrate on initially and how they need to be applied. Make certain everyone understands the approach.

Humans assume wrongly a dog has no sense of numbers. We have found dogs definitely *can* count. In some cases they possess a more acute sense of numbers than their human counterparts. Although mankind likely never will be certain, we believe this probably stems from the fact they watch and listen to their masters or mistresses so intently. If they perceive you really do not mean business until after three repetitions of the word "hup," the dog will not respond until the third time–this, by the way, is not rocket science. Humans can be extremely careless and inconsistent in the way in which they give a command to a dog. Another example of this is to cause the dog to key inadvertently off the wrong command. For example, if you say "hup", "hup", "Fido hup now" then physically make the dog hup, you just taught the dog to hup on the word "now" instead of the word "hup."

We have seen this time and again. For years, a gentile son of Kansas, the quintessential Midwesterner, would make the annual pilgrimage with his beautifully marked liver and white English springer to try his hand at hunt tests throughout the Midwestern states. He invariably had problems with getting his dog into the crate after completing his hunt test events. His approach was predictable, and amazingly consistent. He would give the command "kennel", "kennel" and nothing would happen; the dog stayed out of the crate, but watched the Kansasan intently. Our friend would begin to turn a little red and give the command "kennel" once again. Our springer, true to form, would watch the handler even more intently. The Jayhawker, now purple-faced with veins popping would yell "Kennel! Now!" The dog instantly obeyed and moved with grace and speed into the crate. The man from the Kansas had done a superb job of training his springer to enter his crate on the command "now."

BASIC CRATE TRAINING: This is one of the earliest and most critical commands for which a puppy receives training. If a gun dog trainer does not get crate training down pat, life has a high degree of potential for becoming a living hell. The dog crate is more than a containment system for a gun dog, it is a warm den, a protected area, and a safety necessity when traveling. Done early and correctly, crate training helps house break your dog while conditioning him to spend extended periods of quiet in the crate. This is extremely important for an urban dog owner. When puppies and dogs get a little too rambunctious, when the inevitable dog-shy visitor comes to call, when there is a need for them to be out of the way for a little peace and quiet or sleep, the crate is where they must go.

Crate training starts shortly after a puppy is weaned or when about seven weeks old. At this age, puppies are physically and mentally able to make the transition from the whelping box to a crate. Given the important role the crate will play in both the puppy's life, as well as your family's lives, the crate will become a refuge for you both. Dogs are cave dwellers. They like the peace and quiet of being away from people at times and to be comfy and cozy from the elements while being transported.

Select a crate that is airline approved in one of the standard sizes specifically designed for dogs. It should be constructed of molded plastic, with a good strong handle, and a metal grate door. Place it initially in your bedroom in a place where you will not trip over it in the middle of the night. Resign yourself to spending several sleepless nights. Do not fight it, complain about it, or try short cuts. We have found abject resignation is the key to getting through the crate-training phase. In the long run, your life will be simpler and your dog will be happier for having invested the time up front to do it the right way. One of us recalls fondly the prescription of a really superb pediatrician when his youngest child refused to sleep through the night. "Peach brandy," she said, " a teaspoon for the baby before bedtime, and about five fingers worth in a water glass for you."

Put an old towel with your scent on it in the crate–one sufficiently large to make a nice warm bed for your puppy. If you have just brought the puppy home, you might consider placing an old wind up style alarm clock (it will probably be one that your mother owned given the digital age we find ourselves in) that ticks next to the crate to simulate the heartbeat of the mother. Once you have the crate set up, let your puppy explore the crate. However as bed time approaches, keep the puppy out of the crate and play with him until you are ready to go to bed yourself so as to tire him out.

If you are a typical city person with a traditional working schedule, you will get home between five or six o'clock in the evening and go to bed somewhere between ten or eleven o'clock at night. Feed the puppy before six or seven at night to allow time for him to urinate and

defecate once or twice before bedtime. One key to making a successful night is to pull the water bowl as well as the food bowl a good hour
or two before you go to bed, so that the puppy has voided his bladder
completely before going into the crate. Just before you turn out the
light, put your puppy into the crate saying the word "kennel" and close
the door. This command will mean nothing to the puppy at this time,
but you will begin laying the foundation for a future command.

The first couple of nights will be the toughest. Your new companion
will probably make a fuss for a bit when he is put into the crate; ignore
him, he will get to sleep within ten to fifteen minutes. Plan on getting
up once, maybe even twice in the night to take the puppy outside for a
quick midnight trip to the outhouse. If the puppy starts to whine in the
middle of the night, chances are good he must urinate and he does not
want to soil his crate. Dogs instinctively are clean animals that sometimes go to great lengths not to dirty their dens. Take him out for five
or ten minutes to do his business and stretch a little before going back
to the crate. Within a few days, the frequency of these midnight nature
calls will decline from two times per night, to one, and then to none.

Most puppies adjust quickly to the crate and are doing quite well
after only a week or two of crate training. However, expect field-bred
dogs will quickly learn that if they whine, someone will get up and let
them out. At this stage things can get a little tricky. We are absolutely
convinced that field-bred spaniels and retrievers have a unique ability
to quickly train the gun dog trainer. Use your judgment to determine
whether the puppy really is serious or if he is whining to be let out of
his crate so he can be with you. If you believe it to be the latter, you
have several courses of action. A tried and true method, believe it or
not and successful time and again, is to get out of bed, grab your pillow
and blanket and go lay down by the puppy next to his crate without
opening the door or taking him out. When he whines, whack the crate
on top and say sharply "no" or "stop the noise." A few repetitions of
this and the puppy should cease his whining. Alternatively, assuming
the crate is on your side of the bed (the ever-vigilant spouse usually
demands that it be positioned there), strategically station a couple of
pair of shoes close to your side of the bed. When the puppy whines,
let fly with one of your stockpiled brougham missiles at the crate and

say "no" or "stop the noise." This technique has also proved highly successful in deterring those midnight whines, so much so that the authors wonder if this is the origin of the famous line of shoes called "hush puppies."

Of the two methods, the first is better suited to the preservation of domestic tranquility; if you live alone use the second. In the morning, carry your puppy outside first thing in the morning when you get up so he can relieve himself. Make certain you carry him, as he likely will seek to relieve himself on the carpet directly in front the crate unless you act quickly to prevent it.

In many urban households, there is no one home during the day. If your puppy spends his days in the crate, you need to get home and immediately let the puppy out of the crate, carry him outside and let him relieve himself. Allow your puppy to stretch, run, and romp outside to ensure that he is through with his bathroom chores and to give him a little exercise. Bring the puppy into the house and let him play inside. Spend some time playing–not training–with your puppy. Put yourself in your dog's place. It has been a long day in the crate. To expect a puppy to hold both his bowels and his bladder for eight to ten hours while you have had the benefit of coffee breaks to use the toilet is a lot to ask. However, if you do this correctly, soon your dog will have a bladder and bowels of iron. One cautionary note is in order: *never use the crate as a punishment vehicle.* The crate is a refuge (for you both), not a prison.

As the puppy grows, you will want to not merely put him into the kennel, but to train him to go into the kennel on command. If you have been meticulous in saying the word "kennel" each time you or a family member puts the puppy into the kennel, the job of instilling the command will be all the easier. At two to three months, a puppy is ready to begin to respond to the "kennel" command. We suggest that you throw one of his favorite treats into the kennel and give the command "kennel" to see how the puppy responds. If he goes in reward him with praise and another treat. If the puppy balks at going in, push him gently into the kennel and praise him. Limit the training session to only two or three repetitions.

No and Ahhh! Ahhh!: The Imperatives. This command is a lifesaver both for you and your dog. "No" or "ahhh" (note: if you have small

children, ahhh is a sound that you use naturally to keep them from doing something you wish them not to do; we use them interchangeably)
are commands that needs to be used sharply. When the trainer uses
them, the dog *must in no uncertain terms* act upon them. These "no"
or "ahhh" commands are delivered sharply without a pleasant voice
or facial expression. These commands are used at the very early stages
of a puppy's life. Use this command, for example, when the puppy is
climbing on furniture (unless you want him there), digging up the garden, or doing any act of which you do not approve.

However, for gun dogs, owners should *never, ever* use the "no"
or "ahhh" command while a puppy is carrying an object in his
mouth. It does not matter how precious the thing is–new boots,
children's toys, or undergarments (the only exception to this rule
might be a small thermonuclear device). The retrieving instinct
in field-bred spaniels and retrievers is very strong and you want
to encourage its development. By giving a puppy the "no" or
"ahhh" command while he has something in his mouth, you run
a significant risk of creating retrieving problems downstream.
When faced with this situation, simply take the object out of the
puppy's mouth and give the command to "drop" followed immediately by a "good puppy." One of us recently faced this problem
first hand during a dinner party in which a young English cocker
spaniel playfully retrieved, and carried into the dining room for
all to see, a young female houseguest's thong underwear to the
collective amusement of all (with the possible exception of the
young lady in question). To dissuade or distract the puppy, give
him a rawhide chewie or a rope chew toy (remember–no squeaky
toys). As the puppy matures and focuses his attention on dummies and other retrieving tools, these retrieving *faux paux* will
gradually subside.

The three most essential commands that a dog must learn very early
on are the three H's–*Here, Heel, and Hup.* Once these are mastered,
and they can be mastered early on, they will form the basis of all gun
dog training. We have found the fewer and more ingrained the individual commands, the better for you and your dog.

HUP: The "hup" command (at this point, we will dispense with using the word "sit" altogether and will use the spaniel term "hup" in its stead) forms the basis of so many gun dog commands that it is essential to get this down early–"hup" training can start as early as two months. "Hup" is an essential command for city folks. We assume that most urban gun dogs will live inside the home rather than in an outdoor kennel. To keep your dog from jumping up on you, your spouse, or friends; to stop him from bolting outside when you open the door to buy those three boxes of thin mints from your neighborhood Girl Scout troop; or to settle him down, mastery of the "hup" command is essential. If you elected to buy a puppy, training to "hup" can be started when the puppy is eight weeks old (indeed almost all obedience training can be started at that time). As with all the obedience training detailed in this book, start your training indoors. When your puppy comes running to you push down on its rump either in front of you or along your side and say "hup" repeatedly. You then give the puppy a piece of hot dog or kibble. After your puppy begins to hup on his own, you move to phase two training and say "hup" only once. At this point, your puppy should begin to sit down without you forcing its rump down. If he does not, do not repeat the command, but force his rump down; praise and treat him. Once the puppy is "hupping" well, with your whistle, give him one short pip (we are not talking about a thirty second foghorn-style blast…just a short pip will do nicely) and give him the "hup" command.

Soon your puppy will begin to be conditioned to the whistle as well as the verbal command. This is the beginning of "obedience." Keep lessons short–fifteen minutes at the most–so as not to make training too much of a chore for a young dog, and continue to praise and treat him all through the process. If your dog breaks out of the "hup" position before you give him the release command (as all dogs will do), do not repeat the command. Pick your puppy up and physically place him on the spot where he was "hupped." Do not let him move off the "hup" without a release command such as "here" or "OK." It is not necessary to teach your dog the "stay" command.

It is our belief when dogs hear "hup," they should stay "hupped" until told to do something else or given a release command. Remem-

Bethann Roettger puts this nice young yellow Labrador retriever through his paces. (Photos by Tony Roettger).

ber that young dogs do not have an extremely long attention span. Try not to keep your puppy in the "hup" position for extended periods. A minute may be all he is capable of at this point. However, the ultimate goal is for him to sit at "hup" until released. It makes not the slightest difference if you release the dog a minute or an hour later. Gradually expand the time he sits at "hup" always placing him physically back on the same spot when he inevitably breaks. He should now be ready to move out of doors and be thoroughly trained inside to sit either at the verbal command of "hup" or to one short pip on the whistle.

Now take your dog outside on a checkcord or leash. No doubt, your first impression will be your puppy has lost his mind or forgotten everything you taught him indoors. The outside distractions for field-bred flushing dogs are significant. There are birds, butterflies, toads, frogs, bugs, and leaves galore. The new smells and sounds out of doors are overwhelming. He will want to investigate all of these things, and the farthest thing from his mind is obeying your commands. Indeed, if he were not curious about all of the new sights, smells, and sounds around him, you might want to be more than a little worried about his abilities in the field.

With your canine friend securely held by the leash, give him the "hup" command only once. If he hups, praise him lavishly, give him a nice-sized treat, and count yourself one of the fortunate few. What is more likely is that he will ignore you completely, and you will have to push his rear down. Do not be discouraged or lose your patience, as this is all new to your puppy. With a little work outside of the house, he will come around. Keep using the checkcord or leash during this transition period to ensure that you have absolute control of your puppy. Praise and goodies will work magic. It is extremely important to keep all of your training light hearted and positive with a young puppy; they are, after all much like small children in this regard. Use a happy voice and raise your voice an octave or two. Even if you are a two hundred plus pound knuckle-dragging type of guy (at least one of us can admit to being that body type). It will work wonders for you when you have to actually act like a lion and roar in later training.

HERE: Without a doubt, the most important command for the urban gun dog owner is here. We start this training indoors when the puppy is very young. Puppies very early on naturally run to greet you. When the pup is running to you, all you say is "here" and add your whistle with four or five consecutive pips and treat him with a hot dog sliver or piece of kibble. Your puppy will learn to come when these things are done in repetition. Work on this initially inside your house and continue to treat. If you have a really good hallway or corridor that can be blocked off, start training in this area first. Your puppy will be channeled to you, with no real path for escape. Once he comes to your "here" on a regular basis using praise and treats, move to the more general areas of the house, and from there outside. Also re-enforce "here" training at the puppy's mealtime. While putting the puppy's food bowl on the floor, blow four or five quick pips as the puppy comes to get his food. It is surprising how quickly a puppy will start to respond to the "here" or recall command when used in conjunction with feeding time.

The value of sound "here" training was driven home to us by the following story. Not long ago, one of us, accompanied by his far better half, visited a local park for a leisurely afternoon picnic. As luck would have it, the happy couple, basking in the warmth of a late Spring day, strolled down to the pond, well known for being virtually without any fish, and happened to see a young springer out in the water taking a swim. The spectacle by itself was not particularly unusual, but what was so eye catching about it was the fact that the owner appeared to be fishing while the dog was swimming. Upon closer inspection, it turned out that the dog's owner had a fishing rod and reel with a line attached to the dog's collar and actually was reeling in the dog. According to the owner, the rod, reel, and line system was the only way to allow the dog to swim, and get him out of the water after playtime was over. Obviously, this particular English springer was not well-trained and needed much work on the "here" command.

Ensure you have the indoor "here" command down solidly prior to attempting the same command outdoors. In an urban environment, it is important to have control over your dog at all times. When making the transition from indoors to outdoors, ensure you have your dog on a checkcord (see chapter on equipment) so you can control the puppy at all times and stop it from running into the street or from injuring itself. Use the 30-foot checkcord in combination with treats. Call your puppy to you, and if he comes, give him a treat immediately. If he does not come, reel him in with the checkcord with little tugs (not a haul) and give him a treat. The fundamental principle is consistency in "what" you say and "when" you say it combined with repetition; this is the key to your success. *Do not give a command if you feel that the puppy will not respond to you or you are not in a position to enforce the command.*

Spaniels and retrievers have an uncanny ability, much like children, to know when they can get away with something. Without a doubt, the second you take the checkcord off, your puppy will refuse to respond to your "here" command. These rascals seem to know instinctively they have a newly found freedom to evade your grasp and not heed your command. What do you do when this happens? Making the transition from checkcord to no checkcord can be a little tricky. One technique is for a member of your family or a friend (one your puppy is familiar with) to hold the puppy by the collar while you take out a treat, let the dog smell it, and back away ten feet or so. Signal your friend to release the dog and hold the treat out. Chances are very good the puppy will be straining at the bit to get to the goody as you back up and will fix on the treat immediately after release. Once he comes for it, give him the treat immediately with lavish praise, and repeat several times. Soon he should be coming regularly to you. Spend a lot of time on "here" early on. Concentrate on it until you know your puppy will come to you every time with or without checkcord. Crouch down when giving your puppy the "here" command; *do not bend over* (this also works well when you meet young children). Bending over is intimidating to most puppies. Crouching down in a squat almost always will encourage the puppy to jump on you. Although later this may become a problem (see section on the "off" command), it is essential at the puppy's formative stages that he enthusiastically comes when you call "here." There is time enough much later on to introduce the "off" command.

HEEL: One of the most enduring scenes we have witnessed time and again is the dog handler in many a hunt test, field trial, or hunting situation struggling to control his dog on a lead while waiting to run the dog in the field. The hapless handler, tries desperately to keep his dog under control while his wild-eyed canine companion lunges forward on two hind legs, straining at the lead with forepaws clawing the air in front of him and eyes bulging out of his head. This "spaniel strangle" has been a hallmark of the spaniel (unlike the retriever crowd) American field-bred scene in stark contrast to our colleagues in the United Kingdom. In the past, many American trainers, especially those who have focused on training spaniels for field trials, have not emphasized "heeling" as a key aspect of training for fear of creating a "sticky" dog–one that does not range sufficiently from the handler to cover the field for the gunners. However, for the urban gun dog owner, it is not an option. It is essential that the urban gun dog owner have a dog that heels superbly.

It does not matter to which side you heel your dog. Gun dog tradition holds that right-handed shotgunners heel their dogs to the left, while left-handed shotgunners heel their dogs to the right. The logic here being that the dog does not interfere with the shotgun shooter's mount and swing. Quite frankly, it is a matter of preference, rather than a strict rule. After all, this book is not about training dogs for the show ring, but for the field and life. We have found many trainers teach their dogs to heel on both sides. To make it easier, however, we suggest that you pick either your left or your right and stick with it. In the beginning it is less confusing for you and your dog. Should you wish to teach your dog to heel to both sides later on, it is a relatively easy thing to accomplish.

It is a fundamental fact of nature that dogs do not want to be on a lead. It will take some time (expect this and hope to be surprised) for your youngster to get used to "heeling" with a lead. It does not take a whole lot of gray matter to figure out if you put a slip lead on an eight-week-old puppy, *it will not be heeling by the end of the day*. But this is precisely the expectation of many first time dog trainers. Your puppy will need time to adjust to a lead. A basic obedience or puppy kindergarten class at a local dog school can help you in this area.

We suggest that you initially work your puppy indoors exclusively to preclude the distractions of the outside. Put your dog on a lead and walk next to an indoor wall with your puppy between you and the wall. When your dog seeks to push ahead of you, you say "heel" and merely cut him off at the pass. Do this consistently for two or three weeks for approximately ten to fifteen minutes per night. It may seem like a large investment of time, but it will pay dividends many times over when you are ready to take your puppy outside. Once your friend begins to respond to this, give him the "hup" command while heeling. If he responds, praise him and give him the "heel" command. Do this only once or twice per session. You do not want to overload the puppy at this point in his training.

After your puppy has mastered (a relative term here) the indoor "heel" on a lead, you will want to move him outside. However, with this approach to "heeling" we advocate here, you will want to minimize the amount of outdoor distractions your puppy encounters. Find a fence at a park or playground and use it as you did the interior wall. Heel your puppy along the side of the wall keeping him between you and the wall. Continue to cut him off should he attempt (as he no doubt will) to surge ahead of you. This approach provides specific boundaries for your puppy and reduces the need for choker collars. It also helps preclude the "spaniel strangle" phenomenon.

Once your puppy is trained to heel along a fence, try him out on the sidewalk. He may perform beautifully. He may just as easily strain and pull at the lead. Many would resort to a variety of more severe meth-

Heeling your dog against a wall inside is an excellent drill to prepare for the outdoors. (Photo by Catharine Schleider).

ods than the ones we discussed in the previous section. We have tried them all, the heeling stick (from our British friends), the choke collar, the pinch collar, the halti-collar, the electronic collar....you name it we have tried it. One method that appears to work extremely well is the lash strap method. Take your flat six-foot nylon lead and clip it your puppy's collar. Pull the lead under and behind the left leg, and then cross over your puppy's back to the front of the right leg. Now pull the lead behind the front leg. Heel your puppy, but when he begins to pull and strain at the lead pull *lightly* up on the lead. This method will hobble your puppy without causing him pain, choking him, or frustrating you. Give the command "heel." If he again struggles, pull lightly up on the lead and say "heel" once again as you begin walking. Your puppy can only walk when you release him from the hobble. Keep at it until the puppy begins to understand that when you say "heel" and start to walk, he can only walk with you at the "heel" position. As in everything, praise works wonders. Do not spare the praise, when he "heels."

If you elected to buy a started dog instead of a puppy, you may find that started dogs may have limited "heeling" experience, and may not be sufficiently adept at heeling to pass muster in a city setting. All of the techniques discussed above are equally applicable to started dogs. Some started dogs may even be more of a challenge to teach to heel than puppies–especially if they have had a lot of fieldwork or are extremely "birdy." You will find started dogs will often begin hunt immediately upon going out of doors. These dogs can be a true challenge to teach to heel. Patience, perseverance, and consistency are your greatest allies.

Once you have your new friend walking comfortably at heel, you will find your life has changed for the better. Work with him on the lead for as long as it takes to ensure that he heels smartly each time you give him the command. You will soon find that your puppy will begin naturally to walk at heel with slack in the lead. When this occurs, casually drop the lead without alerting your dog. Let him drag the lead for a while. If he breaks, merely step on the lead and say "heel." Also drape the lead over his back for periods of time. Take your time, but remain consistent. When he is ready and you are fully confident that he will respond and not break off heel, try him off lead. Start inside your home at first, and then progress to the outside. If it looks as if your puppy begins to break off lead, take a step backwards. Put the lead back on him and give it more time. It may seem you are not making progress, but given time, your dog will learn to heel.

Although the "heel" for spaniels (not so for retriever trainers) has been minimized to some extent by those on the American field trial circuit, it is an extremely important part of urban gun dog training. Your gun dog will spend far more time in the city than in the field. You will want to take your dog on walks in parks, playgrounds, and around your neighborhood. Your training to "heel" will be critical to your long-term enjoyment of your gun dog. Moreover, many municipalities have strong leash laws on their books and aggressively cite citizens who violate these laws. We cannot emphasize enough the importance of your dog learning this command thoroughly.

PLACE: An extremely useful command, we have found, is the "place" command. It has been our experience that many urban hunters residing in cities generally pursue a variety of upland game birds and waterfowl. In fact, with today's proliferation of Canada geese (those golf courses really are good for something besides hitting the little white ball) and the successes of conservation organizations such as Ducks Unlimited, you may find waterfowl one of the more available game birds. Spaniels and retrievers both make excellent non-slip retrievers, but they must be trained to perform in the role. Their natural tendency is not to sit quietly in one place waiting patiently for the shotgunner to finally bring one of those fast moving teals down. Instead, they want to be in the field actively searching for game. If you are hunting pheasants, this is just fine; if not, it can be a real nuisance if one is hunting ducks or geese from a blind. "Place" training also is an extremely good precursor to some of the more advanced retrieving drills, such as baseball described in a subsequent chapter, and it will help in beginning the steadying process. It is also about the handiest command you can have when you are eating a really magnificent pheasant dinner with a wonderfully matched wine and you want to do that without the assistance of your four-legged friend at the table.

Start "place" training after your dog has the "hup" command down well, as "place" training in essence is an extension of "hup." Dogs are position-oriented animals; they resonate well with a specific spot–usually your favorite easy chair with all those wonderful smells–but anything that denotes a specific spot will do. We use an old small dishtowel or hand towel as the specific spot. Rub this over your dog so that there is a smell association with the towel. Set the towel down in the middle of the floor. Give your dog the "place" command repeatedly, then pick him up, place him on the towel, give him the "hup" command, and reward him. Remember with each new command you teach your dog, you must start at the first phase then move to the second phase. Once he begins to associate place with the towel, move to phase two. Give the "place" followed immediately by "hup" commands and place him on the towel (if required). Reward your dog with praise and treats.

Once "place" is thoroughly ingrained, substitute the towel for a different one or a small dog bed. The objective here is train your dog to associate "place" with something that you designate, not with a specific object such as a favorite towel or dog bed. Do not let him off the towel until you give him a release command such as "OK." The objective here is to train the dog to sit for extended periods in a duck blind or dove field until you release him for a retrieve. Vary the location of "place" and he will be trained to stay put wherever you set him down.

Once your dog is trained indoors, take a towel outside with the dog on its checkcord. Set the towel down in the middle of the yard (or common area as the case may be), and give the "place" and "hup" commands. Again, if he breaks, do not repeat the command, but set him firmly back on the towel. Do not let him off the towel until you

Left: Hup your dog on a dishtowel inside to start place training. Right: The goal is this! (Photos by Chip Schleider).

release him. Work on having the dog "hupped" on the towel while you walk around (hold onto the checkcord to ensure you can control him if he breaks). Move to progressively larger distances from him. It is important not to call him to you to release him, but instead move next to the dog and say "OK." Later on, this becomes important in teaching a dog to be steady, as he will not anticipate your call to come to you after being "hupped" in the field at the flush of a bird or the sound of a gunshot.

OFF: A very necessary command to preserve the sacred bounds of matrimony as well as one's favorite easy chair is the "off" command. It is an all-purpose command that has many functions ranging from the protection of one's work clothes to safeguarding the sanctity of the marital bed. Spaniels and retrievers, the Lord love them, are absolutely the most adoring creatures in the world (when they are awake). They want to greet you with forepaws planted firmly on your thighs. When this happens, push them away with the command "off", and reward them immediately with praise and stroking. Use the same approach when seated at the table or on the couch. But remember; say "off" only once. If your dog does not respond, physically remove them from the couch, chair, or bed and lavish them with praise when they are back on the floor. A good combination command to give them if you have a dog bed in the room, is to say "off" and follow it with "place." This will take perseverance and consistency on the part of the trainer; the dog will soon learn that you mean business. Nonetheless, do not forget to continue to praise.

ADVANCED HOUSEBREAKING: Housebreaking is perhaps one of the most difficult tasks for a young dog to master. Puppies are naturally reluctant to soil their bedding or crate, often opt instead to leave their "den" piddle in a bedroom, kitchen, or living room. To re-enforce the progress you made while crate training your puppy and to fully house train your dog, you must do several things consistently. While watching television or reading, take pup outside at every commercial break or at approximately twenty-minute intervals, always using the same door to go out to the same area of the yard. This will teach the puppy if he goes to a specific door then he can go outside and piddle. You must always take your puppy out first thing in the morning *before you do anything else*. Again take him out through the same door to the same area of the yard. Always take your puppy *outside the first thing when you get home before you do anything else*. Housebreaking a dog boils down to instilling a strong habit *for both you and the dog*. Once the puppy gains the habit of going outside through a specific door, he will soon learn to go to that door to signal you that he must go out.

There are some additional signals to recognize when a puppy must urinate or defecate. For example, if the puppy begins to act naughty, then chances are good it may have to go outside. Also, if puppy ignores you and begins to sniff around, it likely must relieve itself. Some dogs are very demonstrative as they mature and give clear indications through whining, barking, or standing by the door that they must relieve themselves. Other dogs, the tough ones, are very subtle and give very slight indications that are easily missed when they must answer the call of nature. Both of us own dogs of each type. Learn to read your dog well and your time housebreaking purgatory will be minimal. Again, consistency and anticipation are key elements to successfully housebreaking a young dog.

SOCIALIZATION: Socializing gun dogs for other dogs and humans requires some work and a little thought. It is also one those things that can make one's gun-dog-owning experience in the urban context really memorable, if it is left to chance or not done at all. Puppies are, by nature at birth, gregarious little creatures fond of humans and other puppies alike. They crawl over each other and play in the whelping box together; they are curious, trusting, and above all lovable when held. We cannot really remember a vicious, barking, snapping, snarling, drooling puppy (and we have seen a lot of puppies). About the worst we can recall, is a little puppy teething marks or perhaps a little puppy piddle on the jeans. In short, they are very social little animals from the outset.

Unfortunately, as they grow older, dogs can lose this innocence of puppyhood. Without periodic re-enforcement, a young dog can (not always) become suspicious of strangers and extremely territorial around other dogs. If you have purchased a started dog, it is likely your breeder/trainer has socialized the dog for you. However, some breeder/trainers live in very rural areas. They may have been socialized to other dogs, but human beings are much different. You may have to work a little harder in the area of human socialization. The good news is that socializing dogs to humans and other dogs in an urban setting is not really difficult and there are several ways to go about this. Large pet retail stores often have a "yappy hour" where you can bring your pet with you while you shop. Taking your dog, especially when they are puppies, to pet stores with these policies helps condition them to meeting other dogs and a variety of humans. The astute reader will no doubt recognize that there is a strong correlation between those who frequent pet stores and those who like pets. You are already among those whose sympathies lie with your dog. Obedience classes are also extremely good for socialization; often your local large pet retail store also will sponsor obedience classes.

If you bought a puppy, take him out on walks in your neighborhood, common areas, or in parks to meet as many people as possible. He does not have to be trained to "heel" at this point; the objective here is to introduce your dog to as many different dogs and people as

In a city, there are many opportunities and places to socialize dogs. (Photos by Tony Roettger).

possible through exposure in public places. With a started dog that lacks urban socialization, you need to continually expose the dog to new and varied situations in which people, dogs, and other animals are present. In most cases, people will go out of their way to come over to

admire and pet your dog; most dogs tend to respond positively to this type of attention. However, sometimes we see a shy dog or one that is prone to being territorial. These dogs require a little more work than others, but they almost always come around after a while.

As your gun dog matures, continue with socialization training. Take your dog to a hunt test or field trial with a large gathering of trained gun dogs. At this point you do not have to sign up as participant in either of the two events, but go just to expose your dog to field dogs, owners, and handlers. It is both great fun and an excellent way to further improve your dog's social skills. There is, however, one place we feel is absolutely *off limits* for socializing young puppies–the shooting range. Shooting ranges are the one place where a young puppy can develop a sure-fire case of gun shyness. Take your shotgun and practice; leave the dog at home.

INITIAL RETRIEVING TRAINING: With field-bred spaniel and retriever puppies, there is a strong natural instinct to hold objects in their mouths. Extremely young puppies start carrying things such as socks, underwear, small toys, watches left carelessly on coffee tables–you name it, they carry it. Channeling this effort to retrieve the small canvas dummies discussed in the chapter on equipment indoors are the first steps toward developing the strong retrieving drive so essential in a polished gun dog.

Start basic retrieving training in that blocked hallway or corridor we discussed earlier after your puppy has the "here" command down fairly well. Tease the dog with a small canvas dummy, a small Kong toy, or rolled up sock and throw it a few feet down the hall and call the puppy's name as a release command. Many trainers specializing in retrievers will give the word "back" as the release command. We prefer initially to use the dog's name to prevent confusion in field trials, hunt tests, and hunting situations. Puppy curiosity will cause him to chase the thrown object and pick it up; he may or may not bring it back to you when you call "here." If you hit a home run the first time at bat and your puppy brings it back to you, do not take the dummy from the dog immediately. Instead, with the dummy in his mouth, assuming of course that he has not dropped it of his own accord, praise him extensively verbally and through petting and let him keep the dummy while you do it.

There is no place like a basement for sharpening basic retrieving skills. (Photo by Chip Schleider).

74

Allowing the puppy to keep the dummy for a while after the retrieve helps to prevent the development of possessive behavior in the dog. Later on, a possessive dog will be a hard driver on a retrieve, but when he gets a few feet from you either bypasses you altogether, drops the dummy a yard or so away from you, or will start to duck its head when you reach for the dummy or bird. The longer a young dog keeps the dummy after a retrieve with suitable praise from you, the less likely he will be to develop possessive behavior.

After suitable praise, take the dummy from your puppy using the following technique: grasp the dog on either side of the mouth at the very back of mouth near the jaw hinges using your thumb and fore-finger positioned on different sides of the mouth. Give the command "drop" while squeezing gently and take the dummy. Some puppies or even mature dogs will simply drop the dummy when you say anything. Therefore, you might not have to show a puppy "how" to let go of the dummy. A simple "drop" will often suffice to cause the dog to relin-quish his prize. Make certain that you praise your dog and give him the dummy back immediately by throwing it on the ground or floor. Allow the puppy to chase it and grab it from you in a playful manner. Repeat the process and take the dummy. Give your dog no more than three or four retrieves at the most during this initial phase of retriever training.

Suppose, for example, that your dog chased the dummy, picked it up, but did not come back to you when you called "here." Give him another "here" and go pick him up and take him back to where you were when you threw the dummy. Use the process outlined above to extract the dummy. Have patience, and work on your "here" train-ing without the dummy a little more. Soon, you will find that your puppy will make the retrieve and return to you on both the "here" and whistle commands.

Maturity is a great training tool. Sometimes the best training is no training in certain fields until the puppy has matured a bit. If you are having major retrieving issues at an early age, do not worry about it. One of the worst mistakes a handler can make is to push a dog that is just too young. Often we see this in handlers who are striving for the next level in hunt tests or seeking to get a dog in shape for field trials. Postponing some training to allow a puppy to mature a little is an exercise in common sense. If you encounter problems in one area of training, in this case retrieving, back off, adjust your training plan, and concentrate on improving something the puppy does well.

You may have been working on something for days or even weeks with modest success. Take some time off. Then return to the task the puppy had difficulty mastering, and there is a very good chance that puppy will have improved. This miraculous performance may leave you scratching your head in wonder. Often it is the "maturity factor." Dedication, patience, understanding, knowing when to back off, and taking your time to do it right, but not all of it at once, will, over time, result in major progress.

Once your puppy is retrieving consistently indoors and returning to you with the dummy, you can begin making the transition to real birds by simply attaching a real pheasant or chukar wing to the dummy using duct tape or thick rubber bands. We use the small, soft canvas dummies for the initial phase of this training. Make certain you do this outside the house or in a garage, or incur the undying enmity of your spouse. Be prepared for the possibility that your puppy might seek to tear the wing off the dummy. At this stage they often find that exceedingly entertaining. Do not be overly concerned if that happens; just reattach the wing. However, if he does pull the wing off the dummy take it away so he does not chew on it. You do not want to start a bad habit that can lead to hardmouth. If the puppy continues to pull the wing off and tries to chew it, go back to the plain dummy for a little while, then try again. If the problem persists, seek out a game farm or shooting preserve close to your home and buy frozen quail or pigeons. Use the frozen birds in place of the dummy. If your puppy is retrieving dummies consistently, then the introduction to wings or birds should be relatively easy.

Limit the repetitions of the retrieves so you do not create a situation where the puppy becomes bored with the retrieving game. A great time to stop is if the puppy is begging for one more retrieve. Start out slowly. During one session throw one or two retrieves; in another session throw three or four. Build up the number of retrieves slowly. Puppies, like children, go through stages, sometimes on a daily basis.

If one day your puppy decides not to retrieve, do not force him. Work on something else and come back to retrieves in a day or two. It is far better to not force the issue and run the risk of causing problems that will have to be corrected downstream. An ounce of prevention here is really far, far better than a cure. Whereas indoors you have used dummies, once out of doors, it is time to introduce the puppy to bird wings while continuing to use dummies as well.

Phatlands Northern Skye, MH. (Photo by Tony Roettger).

FIVE

The Basics: Moving From Indoor to Outdoor Training

THE IMPORTANCE OF DRILLS: The term "yard drills' really is a misnomer for an entire family of training drills for gun dog owners that typically require a relatively limited space. Training a gun dog in an urban setting requires a little more precision than this catchall term. Instead, we will just call them drills. If one resides within the limits of a town or city, *drills are the single most important training regime* a city dweller can use to train a gun dog. And a successful transition from indoor training to outdoor training in close proximity to one's home is essential for your puppy's training program. It is difficult to overstate the importance of outdoors drill training at all stages of your dog's life. As your dog progresses through the various stages of training, time and again you will introduce and re-enforce techniques at those training areas closely adjacent to your home.

The urban trainer must apply the concentric circle approach we discussed in Chapter 2 to establishing the proper venue or location for each set of drills. Throughout this book we have sought to organize geographically our training approach. We have started inside the home, moved to the area immediately outside of the home–yard or common area depending upon your personal circumstances–and then moved to public access areas. Drilling is the foundation of gun dog training for the city dweller; therefore, it is extremely important for the urban gun dog trainer to identify an area in close proximity to the home where both dog and trainer can practice undisturbed and without disturbing others. At each new stage of training and with every new task, continually evaluate your dog's progress. Is he ready for the next phase?

LEARNING TO QUARTER: Helping your flushing dog to learn to quarter in the city is a heck of a lot different than in the country. Professionals and adept rural amateur trainers employ a variety of techniques to help those kindergarten puppies to move on to the first grade. Field-bred spaniels and retrievers from good breed stock have a strong instinctive drive to quarter and often need just a little encouragement to begin basic quartering.

Quartering drills may start almost as soon as you bring the puppy home. A very simple drill is to walk in a zigzag pattern as you go outside to get the mail, the newspaper, or if you are just taking the puppy out to answer the call of nature. As you turn to zig or zag, blow two pips on your whistle. After a while, you will find that your puppy will instinctively begin to quarter as you head out the front door. When puppies are seven or eight weeks old they are relatively slow and will have difficulty getting into mischief so long as you are paying attention to them; at this stage they need no real restraint such as a leash or checkcord. Puppies tend to follow a person virtually everywhere until they are approximately twelve weeks old. This, in fact, is one of the main reasons why humans are so incredibly attached to puppies.

After about twelve weeks, puppies become increasingly independent, more adventuresome, and prone to getting into trouble. At this age, start attaching the checkcord to the collar when you go out in the yard or take him out for nature calls. Use the same approach of zigging and zagging with two pips on the whistle as you check out the mail for that latest gun dog supply catalog or evaluate the growth of your garden. At the same time, you can begin basic quartering drills in the park or on your neighborhood playground. You will need an area approximately thirty to fifty yards wide and one hundred yards long–the size of a normal football field or ice rink (depending on what is available to you). Winter is an ideal time for using large playground areas

Fernmoss Jessica, a talented young English cocker spaniel, quarters very well under Tony's control. (Photo by Chip Schleider).

for gun dog training as most children and adults tend to shy away from them during the colder months. Make certain you take your "pooper-scooper" accoutrements with you so as not to leave a mess.

Carefully assess the direction from which the wind is blowing. For this drill, the dog must be quartering almost directly into the wind. While your dog is on the checkcord, "hup" your dog so that he is facing you, otherwise you will be teaching puppy to go straight out. At this point in his training it does not matter to which side you send him out to quarter. The best approach is to send in the direction he is looking. Here we will assume he is facing toward your right. Give him the command "get out," extend your arm to the right and begin moving to your right (note: at the starting position the wind should be blowing directly into your face). If you have done your puppy quartering drills, your dog should be moving to your right out in front of you with the checkcord loose. After moving to the right diagonally as shown in the diagram, blow two pips on the whistle and turn to your left. Your dog should turn with you; if he does not, give him a tug on the checkcord. Move diagonally to your left in a larger version of your zigzag or windshield wiper pattern (in what some call the "drunken sailor" pattern). At each turning position, blow two pips on the whistle. Repeat down the field. When you reach the end of the field, turn around and heel your dog back to the start. You will be moving downwind. At the initial stages of the dog's quartering skill development you should try to keep your dog moving into the wind as much as possible. When you reach your initial starting point, conduct the drill again. Again, limit your sessions to no more than two or three repetitions of the drill to retain the dog's interest. This is a core drill that will serve to help condition the dog to quartering and develop control. Field-bred spaniels and retrievers have a natural instinct to move out in front of you. This drill simply serves to re-enforce that instinct.

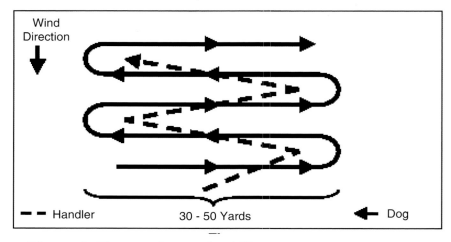

Diagram 1. Playground quartering drill.

RECALL (OR ADVANCED "HERE") TRAINING. At the conclusion of the playground quartering drill lap, introduce recall training. When your dog reaches the end of the field, blow four or five pips on the whistle in rapid succession as the recall signal. Your puppy should by now be conditioned to the "here" or recall signal and come readily to you. If he comes readily to you, reward him lavishly with praise and give him a piece of kibble or sliver of hotdog as a treat. However, if like many young dogs, he gets caught up in the excitement of being outdoors and refuses to obey your command, use the checkcord to reel him in like a fish (a good analogy for how to handle your dog in this situation). For this to be effective, you must "set the hook." Instead of provoking resistance by dragging the dog to you, give the cord a slight "pop" as if lightly setting he hook on a soft mouthed fish, not like a largemouth bass and say "here." This is more of an attention-getting technique than a "haul them in the boat" approach. Praise him and reward him with a treat. In time he will readily come to you. This is also a key element of the playground quartering drill. As your dog matures and you feel sufficiently confident in your ability to recall the dog, you will want to quarter him without the checkcord. When this occurs, it is a product of your training program and the length of time it takes your dog to mature. You will have to be the judge of when you take this step.

THE "QUARTERING" HUP: An important milestone toward training a dog to be steady to flush and shot is reached when the handler can stop a dog hot on the trail of scent and heavily into the thick of the hunt with a single whistle blast. This training also is critical for the urban gun dog. It is essential that you be able to stop your dog on a dime in the city to preclude a dangerous situation from arising for the dog, you, or a third person.

Begin teaching your dog with this drill while still using the checkcord, but after you have been conducting the playground quartering drill for a couple of weeks. Prior to undertaking this, your dog should "hup" readily to a single pip on the whistle. To introduce this to your training, begin by quartering your dog as you have previously. After a couple of turns, blow one short pip on the whistle. If your dog "hups" instantly count yourself as one of the fortunate few, pat yourself on the back, praise the dog lavishly, give him the "get out" command, and resume the quartering drill. It is far more likely, however, that your dog will ignore you completely or seek to return to you as he would on a recall. Should this happen, do not blow the whistle again. Go out to your dog, pick him up, and physically place him on the spot that he was when you gave the command. Praise him and then give him the "get out" command. During the course of your playground quartering drill, give the dog the command only once or perhaps twice during the entire session. If you give the command too frequently during the drill, your dog will begin to anticipate the command, develop a hesitancy in hunting style, and start to look to handler for directions while quartering. This condition is known as "popping." Repeated with minimal frequency over the course of several weeks and months, however, and combined with other outdoors training designed to get your dog to "hup" readily, he will learn to stop on command. Again, do not rush this, be consistent in your corrections, evaluate his progress, and cease this part of the training if your dog begins to "pop."

At this point, you will begin to learn to "read" your dog's responses in a field environment. Dogs react in different ways to commands–some respond instantly to commands and can turn on a dime; others react more slowly. Slow reacting dogs often occur for no apparent reason. It can happen in the quartering process as well as the quartering "hup" process. This is more a delayed reaction than lack of obedience to command. For example, one particular dog that trains at Roettger Ridge Kennel comes to mind. The dog is an extremely talented hunting dog; he is steady to flush and shot and highly trained, but he reacts slowly to commands he is given. When you blow two pips on the whistle to turn him, it takes a full two strides for him to react. He exhibits the same slow reaction times when given the quartering "hup" command. We sought to little avail to correct this problem. In the end, it became obvious that it was just the way the dog responded to the command. Instead of fighting city hall, we compensated and just planned ahead of the need to turn him and gave him two pips on the whistle two strides before he needed to turn. Observe how your dog responds to commands and seek to develop a natural rhythm in your handling of the dog.

OUTDOOR PLACE TRAINING: This is an extension of the indoor place training you undertook in basic obedience training. If your dog is place trained using the small dishtowel approach we discussed in Chapter 4, your dog should be capable of making the transition to outdoors. Take the towel outside and place it on the ground in the yard or common area. While keeping your dog on the checkcord give the "place" command. With all of the outside distractions, he may or may not follow the command the first time. If he does, give him plenty of praise and a treat. If he does not, pick him up and place him in the "hup" position on the towel and again praise him and give him a treat. After a week or so (depending upon your dog) and while still on the checkcord, give him the "place" command, "hup" him, and walk away from him a slight distance. Continue to practice this with plenty of praise and treats when he performs well; pick him up and place him on the towel when he breaks. Gradually increase the distance between you and your dog to where you can "hup" him on the towel and move fifteen to twenty yards away without him breaking. To preclude him from developing what we call the "creeping hup, " never call him to you from his "place." Instead, move to his side and praise him and "heel" to the next training task.

Dixie stylishly demonstrates the outdoor "hupping" drill. (Photo by Chip Schleider).

The purpose behind outdoors "place" training is multifold: to begin to prepare the dog for line steadying, a basic retrieving drill, to condition him to stay next to you in a blind, and to get the dog ready for advanced retriever training. If he does not stay where you place him, he will not be ready for baseball, an advanced retriever drill we will discuss in the next chapter. With consistent practice and patience, he will make significant progress. Ultimately, your goal is to have a dog you can rely upon to sit next to you in a duck, goose, or dove blind, as well as to quarter beautifully to flush upland game for you.

GUNFIRE CONDITIONING DRILLS AND INTRODUCTION TO GUNFIRE: It does not take a lot of common sense to understand a surefire way *to make your puppy gun-shy* is to take him at the tender age of eight weeks to your local gun club and tie him up outside the skeet range. Yet time and again we see the results of just that approach. Once a dog is gun-shy, it is extremely difficult, very costly, and often unsuccessful to try to cure him of the malaise. We recommend a slow, steady, and staged approach to conditioning your dog to gunfire. The approach is so gradual, that when a dog finally hears actual gunfire, he will think that it is nothing out of the ordinary. Start conditioning your puppy when he is eight weeks old. After you have called the puppy to dinner using the four to five pips on the whistle, give him his food and allow him to start eating. Stand far away from the puppy while he is eating and clap your hands loudly once. *Do not do this directly next to your puppy*, but several yards away within earshot and visual distance of the puppy. Initially your puppy will look up at you, but resume eating. Make this a part of your nightly routine for several weeks. *Gradually* close the distance between you and the puppy during the course of this training to within a couple of yards.

After two to three weeks and after the puppy is fully conditioned to the handclap, take out the two blocks of wood connected with the nylon cord that we discussed in Chapter 3. Feed your puppy as usual, but go back to the position where you originally started the handclap routine. When the puppy is eating, clap the pieces of wood together to make a sharp sound. Start out with a sound a little louder than a handclap (you will want to practice a little before you deliver the wood clap), and follow the same routine that you did with the handclap. The objective is for the puppy to become so used to the sound of the wood clap that he barely raises his head from the food bowl. Keep up this nightly routine (note: we feed our dogs in the evening) for several weeks. Modulate the sound of the wood claps. If there is the slightest disturbance in your puppy after a couple of lessons, cease training on the wood clap and return to the handclap. Again, you must be the judge of this and its impact upon your puppy.

Once your puppy is completely comfortable with the wood clap after several weeks of training, you are ready to progress to the next step. Recall our discussion of the children's cap pistol from Chapter 3 (please note that this drill is conducted outdoors to preclude you and the dog from being banished to an outdoor dog igloo as a permanent residence). While on a playful romp outside in your yard or common area and when the puppy is ten yards or so away from you, with the gun held behind your back and pointed toward the ground, fire your cap pistol only once (do not play Wyatt Earp point the pistol at the dog and fire off six caps). If properly conditioned the puppy should look up, but not be unduly startled. If he appears startled beyond looking up at you or flinches in any way, cease training with the cap pistol and resume the wood clap training for a few more weeks. Again, the puppy should respond to the cap pistol sound with curiosity, not anxiety.

Once the puppy is completely comfortable with the sound of the cap pistol after several weeks of training, you will be ready to introduce the puppy gradually to gunfire at a suitable location (game preserve, wildlife management area, hunting dog club, etc.). We accomplish the introduction to actual gunfire as gradually as we did all other phases of gunfire conditioning training. While the dog is quartering out in front, have a friend fire a single shotgun shell in a safe direction ten to twenty yards away from the dog with the barrels pointed away from the area in which the dog is quartering to reduce the noise (and save the dog). At this point, the dog should be approximately sixteen to twenty weeks old; if you have done all proceeding steps correctly and not rushed the dog, there should be no visible reaction on the part of the dog. If you combine this introduction to gunfire with some work on birds, you will find the dog may be so intent on finding and flushing birds he fails to notice the gun shot altogether (see the section below on introduction to birds). Repeat this exercise several times during the training session, always taking care not to be too close to the dog when the shotgun is discharged, and you will find that the dog is fairly well conditioned to gunfire at this point. From here on, use common sense with the shotgun and *never, ever* discharge the gun in close proximity to the dog. There is no guarantee that a dog will not be gun-shy. Some dogs have a genetic predisposition toward gun-shyness that these drills may do little to mitigate. However, if you follow the steps carefully, your dog's introduction to gunfire should be relatively smooth and should not frighten him.

Chip gives Dixie a "line." (Photo by Catharine Schleider).

Basic Marking, Lining, and Retrieving: Your puppy should be ready to begin basic marking, lining, and retrieving drills when he is approximately four to six months old. Again, you must evaluate his maturity level; it is possible to start these earlier, and it is also possible that he will not be ready until he matures a little more. The retrieve is so important to the inner workings of a good gun dog because, if the dog retrieves well, you can teach him virtually any gun dog skill. The retrieve becomes the reward for accomplishing specific tasks. We have seen line steady dogs doing thirty to forty yard marked retrieves

Bethann works on initial outdoor retrieving (Photos by Tony Roettger).

at the age of twelve weeks and puppies that are eight to nine months old not wanting to deliver the bird. Remember dogs are individuals and will develop a strong retrieving drive at different times. A good rule of thumb is if he is carrying objects in his mouth consistently, it is generally safe to undertake more rigorous retriever training. Take your time, and let his retrieving develop before undertaking more advanced retriever training.

After your hard work indoors and outdoors on initial retriever training, your puppy (now rapidly becoming a dog) should be ready to undertake more advanced retrieving drills designed to improve his bird marking ability. Introduce him to lining, and sharpen his ability to make increasingly longer retrieves. Up until now, your dog has had relatively short and simple retrieves of roughly twenty to thirty yards at most. We now want to begin to expand the distances while teaching the dog how to take a "line" to the dummy. Your dog is not yet "line steady" which means he will stay "hupped" at your side when you or another person throws a dummy for him and he will still be on the checkcord so that you can maintain control of him. Carefully gauge his

89

progress at this point. If you have doubts about your ability to recall him, you might want to postpone moving to these drills.

To begin, "hup" him at your side and place your foot on top of the checkcord to restrain him. Toss the dummy about thirty yards in front of you simultaneously blowing one pip on the whistle. At this point your dog, conditioned to leap at the slightest throw of the dummy, no doubt will spring forward only to be checked in his advance by the pressure of your foot on the checkcord. "Hup" the dog again while keeping your foot on the checkcord. While the dog is "hupped" extend your hand over the top of his head toward the dummy without blocking his view. This is known as giving the dog a "line" or direction to the mark. Later during advanced retriever training you will throw doubles and triples. Because you have taught him to "line" the dummy early on, he will use your directional hand signal to pick up whichever dummy you want him to retrieve first. Make certain you have taken your foot off of the checkcord and call the dog's name as the release command while still holding your hand in the direction of the retrieve. Since you have trained him since puppyhood to associate his name with the retrieve, he should bolt off the line and make the retrieve. Once he has the dummy, immediately give him the recall command unless puppy comes to you on his own. If the puppy comes to you without recall, save the command for when you need it. Less is better in this instance. If he does not bring it directly to you, haul him in on the checkcord using the "set the hook" approach we discussed previously. Remember, give a slight pop on the checkcord, blow four or five pips on the whistle, and give the "here" command. Be careful not to pull so hard on the checkcord that the puppy spits out the dummy–an obvious set back and counterproductive to the goal. If the puppy runs away from you, slow him down, but do not jerk him with the checkcord. This is dog training not rodeo calf roping. When the puppy comes in, praise him as always and give the dog a treat.

Practice this drill for two to three weeks and you should begin to notice that his lunges are less frequent or disappear altogether. He will increasingly become steady to the thrown dummy and will begin to associate the line of your hand with the mark of the retrieve. A good handling tip with your dog is to drop down on one knee and focus your attention on the ground immediately in front of the *dog without looking directly into the dog's eyes*. We have found that often as a young dog or puppy approaches the handler with his prize securely in his mouth, he sometimes will shy away from delivering the bird to the handler if the handler is standing and looking directly at the dog. Stay on one knee with your dog until he is delivering the bird or dummy to your hand. At the point that he is steady without your foot being on the checkcord, the dog is ready to move to the next step.

Tony demonstrates the over-the-shoulder dummy toss, a key step in line-steadying your dog (note: his body is between the dog and the dummy). (Photo by Chip Schleider).

INTRODUCTION TO WATER: The timing of a puppy's introduction to water depends on two variables in the dog-training equation–age and the season of the year. We like to begin the introduction to water when the puppy is about four months old and has a highly developed retrieving drive. However, this depends heavily upon the season of the year. A good way to think about this is to put yourself in your dog's shoes or paws as the case may be. If your parents had insisted upon you learning to swim in the dead of winter and your first introduction to this was having your father pick you up by the scruff of the neck and heave your body into the frigid waters of a pool or neighborhood pond, it is possible that you might have second thoughts about going in after sputtering and thrashing as you made your way back to shore. Similarly a mid-winter sink or swim approach could have a disastrous affect upon your newly minted retriever.

A nice water retrieve through cover by Marshbanks Weekend Warrior JH WD owned by John and Jenny Durand. (Photo by John Durand).

Wait until the weather is mild, the water temperature is warm, and the dog's drive to retrieve is strong before introducing your puppy to water. Dogs are natural swimmers, and given the strong incentives of retrieving a dummy or bird, they readily adapt to the water. There are a couple of very good methods to accomplish the introduction to water. Depending upon your circumstances and proximity to water you might consider one or the other. The first method works well if you live in an area that is close to modest amounts of water–such as municipal ponds. On a warm sunny day, take your dog to the pond with his favorite retrieving dummy (be prepared to get wet yourself and dress accordingly). In a shallow portion of the pond that has a small shelf or gradual slope, tease your dog with a dummy and get him very excited. When he is begging for the dummy, toss it in the water about a foot from the shore, but within easy reach of your dog. He should be able to retrieve the dummy, but will have to get his feet wet, but not swim, to make the retrieve. In all likelihood, the dog will be somewhat hesitant and may require some coaxing to get into the water. Keep enthusiasm in your voice and the excitement level up for your dog. As long as there is some solid ground, he likely will get his feet wet to retrieve the dummy. When he makes the retrieve, praise him and give him another retrieve of the same distance; repeat this two or three times at the most. If he is hesitant, *do not throw him in*. Continue to encourage him to retrieve the dummy. If he still does not retrieve the dummy, pick it up yourself, and place it on the bank partially in the water so he can make the retrieve, but still get his feet wet. Persevere with this and continue to entice the dog into the water with the dummy. It may require more than one visit to the pond to get him to go into the water a foot or so from the shore.

A short retrieve from shore helps build the dog's confidence in learning how to make water retrieves. (Photo by John Durand).

Once you have him walking into the water to retrieve the dummy a foot or two from the bank, toss the dummy a very short distance, three or four feet at most, from the bank to where the dog will have to swim very, very slightly to make the retrieve. Be prepared to get a little wet yourself to retrieve the dummy if he balks and refuses to swim the short distance to make the retrieve. Keep at it. Ultimately the dog will swim to get the dummy; when this happens do not be stingy with the praise. Gradually increase the distances of the retrieve a foot or so at a time, but keep the number of retrieves per session low–no more than three or four.

The second method, we call "take a hike," requires ready access to streams or beaches. Again you must be prepared to get wet and dress accordingly. This approach takes advantage of a young dog's natural playfulness and willingness to follow you. The term "take a hike" conveys exactly that approach. On a nice warm, sunny day take a walk with your dog along the beach, if you happen to live along or close to the coast, or in an area with shallow streams. Walk through shallow water that both you and the dog can easily walk through without having to swim. Make this a fun exercise, be playful, romp, and wrestle. The dog should follow. Gradually move to deeper water still playing and romping. The dog should have to jump through the water, but still not have to swim. After playing this way for a while, move to water where he must swim only slightly to get to you. When he does, make certain to reward him with praise. Gradually, move to water where he must swim to get to you. This may take more than one outing. Be patient and do not seek to shortcut the method by tossing your dog into the drink. Water work is a matter of confidence building for the dog. The more you both practice, the greater the dog's confidence, and the greater the distance he will swim to make those classic water retrieves so characteristic of truly well trained spaniels and retrievers.

INTRODUCTION TO BIRDS: The astute observer will notice that we have led the urban gun dog trainer through almost five full chapters of obedience and gun dog training drills without the use of birds. This, no doubt, flies in the face of current flushing dog training philosophy that places a heavy emphasis upon getting dogs on birds as soon as possible. If the trainer possesses the facilities for maintaining birds and training dogs, then, by all means, training dogs on birds may start as early as the trainer believes the dog is prepared for bird work. However, most city dwellers will not possess the facilities for maintaining birds or ready access to fields that allow for their use in training. With that in mind, we have developed an approach for urban residents that should enable them to undertake preliminary bird training.

Resources the urban gun dog trainer needs to capitalize on are: gun dog clubs, professional trainers, and game preserves in close proximity to one's home. All of these can provide the urban trainer with access to birds and training facilities that allow for the use of birds. If you are fortunate, there will be a hunting spaniel or a retriever club (remember non-slip retrievers are trained quite differently from flushing dogs) sufficiently close to where you live to allow you to participate in club training days. Generally a club's training days are held on a game farm, and include basic instruction on dog handling, bird work, and retrieving. They are superb resources for the city-bound trainer.

If you have rung the gong with the wooden mallet at the county fair, you will live reasonably close to a professional trainer. Professionals routinely conduct hour long training sessions that include birds and normally allow the gun dog owner to "pay by the drink." There is really no better way to get your dog up to speed than through an hour or so of professional training (see Chapter 7 for more information on professionals). If you do not have ready access to a gun dog club or professional training facilities, there is a good chance you may live close to a hunting preserve. Hunting preserves have become so popular in recent years; there is hardly an urban area in the United States that is not within an hour's drive from one. Consult *Black's Wing & Clay*, which annually updates and publishes a detailed listing of hunting preserves by state. They also maintain a website, in addition to the hard copy book. Often hunting preserves will allow you to purchase birds and may offer you access to some training areas for a fee. If you strike out on hunting preserves close to where you live, you can also trap feral pigeons using commercially available traps from gun dog catalogs and online supply stores.

We start dogs on birds, initially using pigeons, in the following way. If the dog already retrieves dummies very well and is comfortable re-

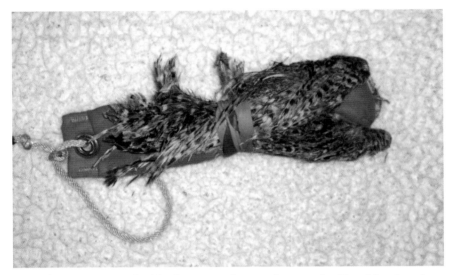

A dummy wrapped with pheasant wings and secured with rubber bands provides a good alternative to birds in retriever work. (Photo by Chip Schleider).

trieving wings or "winged dummies" the transition to birds is relatively straightforward. Start with a dead or frozen bird and toss it as if it were a dummy. This will appear as a normal retrieve and your dog should run to the bird, scoop it up, and return to you out of habit. However, some dogs will run to the bird and hit the brakes. The dog likely will give the bird a good sniff and gingerly pick the bird up by the head or a wing. This second example is extremely common when dogs first encounter birds. Some dogs will very naturally just grab hold of the body; most dogs will have to learn to carry the bird properly. Approach the retrieving of birds as you do dummies. A word of caution probably is in order here. We have found that some dogs, but not all, will start to retrieve only birds and will stop retrieving dummies once more serious bird work starts. If this happens, then you probably are stuck with using birds from this point forward in the training. If the puppy will no longer retrieve dummies but will retrieve birds, do not force the issue. Keep trying the dummies from time to time. Sometimes, especially if there is a lag between when a puppy had his last bird, he will begin to retrieve dummies again. Remember the ultimate goal is for your dog

to retrieve birds, so do not be overly concerned. The most that this will do is complicate your training.

The next step is to introduce the dog to clipped-wing pigeons. This will require a couple of pigeons and a game farm or wildlife management area location in which to train. There are two primary methods of properly clipping a bird's wing. The first method is to pull the flight feathers out of one wing. This makes the bird virtually flightless, but it will continue to flutter and will be capable of flights of very short distances, approximately thirty yards or so, with a toss and a good wind at its back. The problem with removing flight wings, however, is that the bird is permanently unable to fly. This style of clipping a pigeon's wing means that you will be more limited in the training uses to which you put the bird. A more useful method that allows for multiple bird uses, assuming the dog does not kill the bird, is the tape method that employs standard masking or electrical tape. Take a small piece about two or three inches long and tape up all the flight feathers on one wing. The tape will hold them all together, make the pigeon unstable in flight, and turn the bird into "flapper."

Once you have sufficiently flight-hobbled the bird, grasp the body of the

a. Sequence of turning a bird into a "flapper." (Photos by Chip Schleider).

97

bird and hold it head down. Spin your wrist rapidly in a clockwise motion to dizzy the pigeon and plant him in a field under a clump of grass downfield from where you will begin to quarter your dog. Learning to dizzy the pigeon properly will take a little time and practice. Plant the bird in minimal cover. When planting dizzied birds, walk straight down the outside edge of the field tossing dizzied birds into the center of the field as you proceed downfield. Using the approach will help prevent your dog from trailing your path straight down the middle of the field instead of quartering. We have found dogs tend to be much smarter than humans give them credit for being. Make certain your dog stays in the crate facing away from you while you plant birds. Conduct your playground quartering drill as previously described in this chapter. Your dog should find and flush the bird. Allow your dog to retrieve the clipped-wing once flushed to condition him to retrieving live birds. Practice this drill several times with the dizzied clipped-wing pigeons. When you have finished with the pigeon, you may take the tape off and use the pigeon as a flyaway bird to practice your "gone aways"–provided the bird is still alive.

Gone Aways: We believe early in a dog's training, you need to introduce the "gone away" command–starting as early as eight to twenty weeks, but after the puppy has been introduced to birds. This command is extremely important, because as a handler, you will not want your dog chasing flushed but not shot birds into the next county. If pheasant hunting in South Dakota is your ultimate objective, the "gone away" command will keep your young friend from flushing every pheasant in his path as he chases that rooster you missed or a hen you could not shoot.

We prefer the traditional British command of "gone away" to "no bird," because we believe that "no bird" carries with it an negative association, the "no" portion of the command, with birds, which we obviously want the dog to associate with positively. To teach the command, start by planting a pigeon that has not been permanently made into a clipped-wing bird. If you used the tape method to temporarily flight-disable the pigeon, remove the tape, dizzy the bird as you did previously and plant the bird down field in light cover. Start the dog quartering. When he finds and flushes the pigeon *say nothing and give no commands*. The puppy will soon tire of chasing the bird, and when he does he will turn to look at you. *Then and only then*, give the command "gone away" and give the recall command of four to five pips on the whistle. When he comes to you, make a big fuss over him with a lot of praise. Timing is critical to success in "gone away" training. Also crucial in teaching this command is waiting until the puppy slows down and turns before giving the command. If you incorporate "gone away" training each time you work with birds, over time you will instill in your dog the control necessary to keep him from chasing wild flushing or missed birds. It greatly simplifies the steadying process we discuss in the next chapter.

PUTTING IT ALL TOGETHER: Once you are comfortable with his ability to tolerate gunfire, quarter, flush, respond to the recall whistle, and handle basic "gone aways," it is time to put it all together. To do this you will need some help. If you have taken our advice and joined a hunting spaniel or retriever club, enlist the help of a couple of club colleagues for this training exercise. You may wish to attempt it in concert with a club training day where you will find a veritable legion of helpers. If you elected not to join a club, draft a couple of your hunting buddies (luring them with promises of barbecue and beer has worked wonders to overcome an initial reluctance of some to dedicate part of a Saturday to dog training). In any case, you will need a couple of gunners to help you with this drill so you can concentrate on handling the dog and not the shooting of the birds. You will also need a suitable wildlife training area that permits dog training and pigeon use with gunfire (see Chapter 2).

Plan your course so that it is roughly a football field size area with light to moderate cover. If at all possible, try to plan the course so that you will quarter your dog into the wind. We recognize that Mother Nature never really has dog trainers in mind when on Saturday mornings she does not neatly align wind direction with field layout, but do the best you can to enable the dog to quarter as much into the wind as possible. Dizzy and plant three pigeons about twenty yards apart downfield from one another in a zig-zag pattern. Use figure 1 as a guide and plant the birds where the handler would normally turn, not at the extreme outside limits of your dog's quartering pattern. With your gunners posted approximately twenty yards to your left and right in a line with you, hup your dog facing you and give him the "get out" command to start him hunting.

Concentrate on how your dog hunts and move down the field with the dog, keeping the gunners on a line with you. The dog should be quartering out to roughly the position of the gunners before you turn him. Your dog should make its first contact fairly quickly, flush the bird, and if you have chosen your gunners well, they will make the shot. Although your dog is not steady to flush and shot yet, give him his name as a release command (he probably will be well on the way to making the retrieve on his own). Recall him, drop to one knee, and do not look him directly in the eyes as he returns to you with the prize. If you are lucky, he will retrieve the bird directly to hand; he also may only bring the bird within a yard or two of you. Do not reach for the bird first, but let him hold it. Praise him to the high heavens, and then take the bird. Continue down the field and flush the next two birds. Keep the lesson short. Three birds are more than enough the first time out. Keep practicing this on weekends. We recognize that this is tough for the city dweller, but even if you are only able to get in three or four sessions in as many months, the dog will make progress.

Line Steadying: This is an essential step toward advanced gun dog training. By now your young charge should be capable of performing gun dog tasks at what essentially corresponds to the AKC Junior Hunter level (see Chapter 8 for a discussion of hunt and field tests). He should quarter, be able to flush birds, mark and retrieve shot birds from land and water at a variety of distances, and hunt under control. To get him to the next level of performance and capable of performing the drills outlined in the next chapter, he will have to be line steady. You have already introduced the basics of steadying through the marking, lining, and retrieving drills and the outdoor "place" training drills. In line steadying you will build upon this foundation.

"Hup" the dog and move away from him about ten to fifteen feet. Face the dog, take a dummy and tease the dog with it, and throw it over your shoulder while carefully maintaining your body position between the dog and the dummy. At the same time you blow one pip on your whistle. Chances are good that he will race toward the dummy even after you blow the "hup" command on the whistle. Do not allow the dog to make the retrieve if he breaks. Instead, place him back on the spot where he was when you gave him the whistle command and place him in the "hup" position. Once in this position, give him his name as the release command and allow him to make the retrieve. Praise him suitably, and repeat the process. Ultimately with practice, patience, and time, he will become steady to dummies thrown in this fashion. When you are confident that he will not break, begin throwing while he is moving around normally in the yard. Again, give one pip with the whistle to "hup" him, and then send him off for the retrieve by calling his name. Remember in the beginning stages of line steadying to throw the dummy behind you so that you can catch the dog if he breaks. The key is to not allow him the reward of the retrieve if he breaks; by always keeping your body between the dog and the dummy, you are always in a position to preclude him from making the retrieve should he break. Do not worry about marking the fall yourself; the dog will do that part. Pay attention to the dog. Once he is steady as a rock on dummies thrown behind you, proceed to throwing off to the sides. Eventually you will be able to throw the dummy in front of the dog and not have him break.

When fully trained in this fashion, he should begin to "hup" on his own whenever he sees *a dummy in flight*. We mean this last line literally. The objective is to have a puppy that "hup" to dummies and birds while they are in the air. Do not stop the dog until the dummy is thrown, and do not stop the dog and then throw the dummy. You are training the dog to ultimately be steady to *flush and shot*. Remember, the bird must still flush before you are able to train the dog to be steady to shot. At this point, he is ready to move on to more advanced training.

Advanced line steadying drill (note: Tony's body position relative to the dog and the dummy). (Photo by Chip Schleider).

SIX

Advanced Urban Gun Dog Training

As in the previous chapter, the bulk of your training will be done outside the home, except for times in which you wish to work on obedience drills and other non-rambunctious training that can be accomplished indoors during inclement weather. Prior to embarking on the training contained in this chapter, your dog must be fully capable of performing all of the drills in the previous chapter and be absolutely line steady. If you are not convinced your dog is prepared to take on these more advanced training tasks, stay with the drills and the training approach we outlined in Chapter 5. Remember there is *no set timetable* to which a dog must adhere. Many a trainer has created more problems than he or she has solved by pushing a dog that was simply not ready to proceed to the next level. Carefully assess your dog's progress and capabilities prior to moving on to the next level at every phase of training. In gun dog training, slow and steady really does win the race. Because a dog matures more slowly, does not indicate he is either good or bad. The key is to work at the dog's developmental pace to get the most out of him.

ADVANCED RETRIEVER TRAINING DRILLS: In the preceding chapters we covered initial and basic retriever training. By now your dog should be retrieving both birds and dummies well and directly to hand. (if by now your dog is not retrieving directly to hand, you may wish to seek the advice of professionals). We introduced the basics of marking, lining, and basic water retrieves–the bare necessities a dog needs to successfully participate at the AKC Junior Hunter level in hunt tests. In this chapter we will provide you with tools necessary to help you make a polished retriever out of your gun dog. We need to caution the reader at the outset that one is not going to take his or her dog to this level overnight. We also want to make it clear that English springers and English cockers do not behave like a Labrador or a golden retriever. They often have an extremely strong innate quartering drive that increases in strength as the dog matures. This is not to say these spaniel breeds cannot excel as retrievers–this is not the case at all. Spaniels are often some of the most dynamic, capable, and downright beautiful retrievers of the sporting dog world. What we mean here is that *spaniels behave and learn differently than retrievers.* Spaniels often have a far "softer" personality than the retriever breeds and some non-slip training in some cases are too harsh and boring for spaniels or the softer retriever breeds. This all boils down to the fact that you need to carefully gauge your spaniel or retriever breed type in meeting your retrieving objectives.

By now your young flushing dog is a fairly capable retriever. He should be retrieving dummies and shot birds from ranges between twenty and fifty yards, His retrieves should be, if not to hand, in fairly close proximity to you. He should retrieve enthusiastically, and, if all has gone reasonably well so far, you should be able to use the retrieve itself as a reward. This last part is a necessary condition if you are seeking to progress to more advanced levels of retriever work.

The next phase of retriever training is what we call the simple cone drill. This drill is designed to develop the dog's confidence in his ability to make unmarked retrieves, set the stage for him to do blind retrieves, develop his lining skills, and cement his trust in your ability to also provide him a bird to retrieve when you send him out. We owe a debt of gratitude to Jim Spencer, D.L. and Ann Walters, and Pam Kadlec for many of the advanced retriever drills we discuss in this section. These dedicated professionals have worked to identify sound retriever development techniques particularly applicable to flushing dogs. Take one of the traffic cones you purchased at your local sporting goods store (see Chapter 3) and place it in light cover or on a lawn (see figure 2). Pick up three dummies and take your dog on heel to the cone. Place the three dummies on the ground in front of the cone with each dummy separated by a couple of feet. Make certain your dog has seen you place the dummies on the ground, and heel him to a point approximately fifteen feet from the cone.

"Hup" him at your side facing the cone to set him up for the retrieve. While he is "hupped," indicate with your hand a "line" over the top of his head toward the pile of dummies without obscuring the cone. Make certain he has his attention focused on the cone, and send him for a retrieve using his name as a release command or, alternatively, you can give him the command "back." Upon being released, he should head directly for the dummies arranged in front of the cone. If he does not head toward the cone, but breaks right or left, or acts confused, place him back on the lead and heel him to the dummy pile. Pick up one of the dummies and toss it in front of the cone. Heel him back to the start position and start over. He should retrieve the first dummy. When the retrieve is complete, set him up for the second and then the third retrieves. He may take the first and second and forget the third. In any case, keep practicing over the course of a week or two you will find that he has begun to associate the cone with the dummies without a toss of the dummy for him to mark. It is essential that during this training period you keep the cone and the dummies in the same place. After he is fully comfortable with the drill, and is routinely delivering dummies to you, remove the cone, but continue to show him the placement of the dummies. After he is fully capable of retrieving the dummies on the basis of the line your hand indicates to the target, place the dummies in their usual spot without him seeing you do so. See if he is able to make the retrieves solely on the basis of your hand direction. This drill has many different variants. For example, you may wish to leave the cone in place but increase the distance of the retrieve from fifteen yards, to thirty, fifty, and more. This will help your dog associate your lining direction with a retrieve no matter how far out the bird is. Stay with the simple cone drill for a month or two playing out various aspects of the drill to improve your dog's confidence in your ability to always indicate through your hand signals the location of the bird.

When you feel that your dog has thoroughly mastered the simple cone drill, try the advanced cone drill. Lay out a course as depicted in figure 3. Establish a base position from which you and the dog will start all retrieves. Use an imaginary watch to help you.

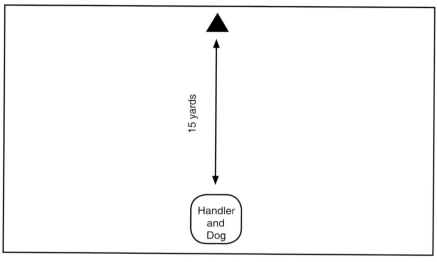

15 yards

Handler
and
Dog

Diagram 2. Simple Cone Drill.

Face the twelve o'clock position (noted on the diagram as 2) and pace off roughly fifty yards and plant a cone. Return to start and this time face the nine o'clock position (noted in the diagram as position 1). Again pace off fifty yards and plant a cone; return to start. Face the three o'clock position (noted in the diagram as position 3), pace off fifty yards, and plant a cone. For this drill you will need six dummies. With your dog at heel, walk to position 1 and place two dummies. Return to start; from the start position walk to position 2, place two dummies, and return to start. Do the same for position 3.

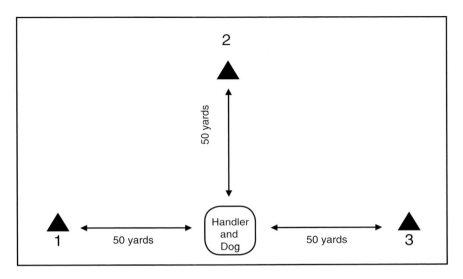

Diagram 3. Advanced Cone Drill.

To perform the advanced cone drill, stand in the start position facing position 1, "hup" your dog at your side and give him a line to the first cone. Give him his release command to send him out for the retrieve. If he runs the fifty yards and makes the retrieve, you can count yourself lucky and praise him extensively. It is far more likely, however, that he will reach the twenty to thirty yard mark and start hunting for the dummy. This is the direct result of the inherent limitations of your throwing arm. Heretofore, you have had the dog retrieving primarily thrown dummies. He is used to making retrieves within the twenty to thirty yard range. If you have conducted the simple cone drill with varying distances as we suggested in the previous section and have conditioned the dog for retrieving dummies beyond your normal throwing range, then it should be not be a significant problem. To overcome this, move closer to the cone and resend the dog for the retrieve. While the dog is heading toward the cone, back up to the start position so that he will have to run the entire fifty-yard distance to give you the dummy. Repeat this several times to condition him to the longer distances. Ultimately he will make the fifty yards out and back. It may take more than one training session, but remember patience is the key in honing retriever skills.

Once he is retrieving routinely from fifty yards at the first cone, turn toward the second cone, give him a line, and send him out for the retrieve. He should take the line at this point. However, sometimes he will still have the memory of the first bird and may turn left and head toward the first cone. If this happens, let him proceed a little ways toward the cone, about ten or fifteen yards, "hup" him and recall him. Line him up again for the second cone and send him out. It may take a couple of tries, but ultimately he will line for the second cone. After he makes the retrieve, praise him as allows, turn to your right and line him up for cone number three. Once the retrieve is made, start over on cone number one and proceed again through the rotation.

After he is completely comfortable with making retrieves at fifty yards in three different directions, mix up the pattern of the retrieve. Start with cone number two, move to number one, and then try number three all with the cones still in place. After mixing up the retrieve pattern for a while, try removing the cones. If you have not changed the layout of your course, he should be capable of making the retrieve at fifty yards without the cones to aid him in all directions that you indicate. This is a major step toward training him for the blind retrieves we discuss a little later on in this chapter. Remember, be extremely consistent in how you give the dog line. Watch his eyes and body position to ensure that it is lined up for the retrieve to preclude him from taking an incorrect line to the dummies.

Once you have him routinely lining and retrieving at fifty yards, you may now proceed to the baseball drill. Baseball provides an almost infinite variety of drills that you can perform to help train your dog to take directions in the field on blind retrieves and to improve his retrieving ability. It also has the added plus of helping him to become steady to flush. You can make it stationary, moving, incorporate long retrieves, blind retrieves, or concentrate on short retrieves. In short, it is perhaps the best single drill you and your dog can do to sharpen his overall retrieving skill set. Before you can undertake the drill, however, your dog must be totally steady to thrown dummies.

Diagram 3 shows the layout of the baseball drill. In a relatively spacious open area, place your dog on the pitcher's mound of an imaginary baseball diamond and "hup" him. Stand on home plate, take out a

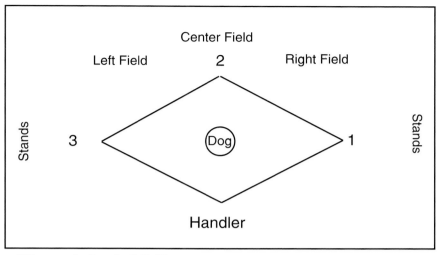

Diagram 3. Baseball Drill.

dummy, and throw it to an imaginary first base approximately thirty yards from your position re-enforcing the "hup" with a single pip from the whistle to ensure that he does not break. If he breaks or creeps in the direction of the dummy, seek to head him off before he makes the retrieve. If he has picked up the dummy, take it from him, place the dummy on the ground (do not say "no"), and physically carry him back to the pitcher's mound where you resituate him in the "hup" position. If the dog is truly line-steadied, he will have tracked the course of dummy, turned toward the dummy on first base, and remained in the "hup" position. Get his attention; you may have to blow one pip on the whistle, so that he physically turns toward you. Once you have his attention, extend your hand to the right, and give him the command "over" to release him. He may not release, as it is the first time he has heard this command. If this is the case give his name as the release command followed by the word "over." He should make the retrieve and bring you the dummy. Reposition him on the mound and place yourself at home plate and repeat the drill.

Concentrate on one base at a time. After he is retrieving well from first base, switch to throwing to third base. Again throw the dummy, and make certain he remains steady by blowing a single pip on the

Tony gives a "back" command to Jessica. (Photo by
Chip Schleider).

whistle. After gaining his attention, extend your left arm toward the
dummy and give the "over" command. He should make the retrieve
handily. "Heel" him over to the mound and repeat the drill. So far
you have taught him a right over and a left over. It is now time to
teach him the "back" command. Again with the dog "hupped" on
the pitcher's mound, toss the dummy directly over his head to second
base. He will no doubt turn to mark the fall. With one pip on the
whistle turn him toward you.

Once you have his attention, extend your right arm straight up in
the air, and give him the command "back" followed by his name if the
"back" command does not release him for the retrieve (you will soon
dispense with using his name as a release command in this drill once
he has mastered the commands of "over" and "back"). He should
head straight for the dummy and make the retrieve. Practice these
individual base drills for a week or so until the dog has them down
perfectly. Dogs generally have fewer problems on "overs" than they
do with "backs," so you may wish to allocate your practice repetitions
accordingly.

By now your budding Ted Williams should be retrieving dummies from first, second, and third base with minimal difficulty. It is time to introduce some complexity to the drill with multiple retrieves. In this case, you will start out with a double retrieve and move to triples. In double marked retrieves, the first bird thrown is called the *memory* dummy or bird and the second is called the *diversion*. When you progress to three dummies thrown, the first two are the memory dummies while the last dummy thrown is called the diversion bird. "Hup" the dog on the mound and throw a bird to first base and then throw one over his head to second base. Second base is the diversion bird and the one that he will focus on. Give him a pip on the whistle to gain his attention, and then give him a "back" to initiate the retrieve accompanied as always by the proper hand signal. He should make the retrieve and return to you with the dummy. Again "hup" him on the mound and return to home plate. Now give him an over to first base with your right arm extended out from your body. He should make the retrieve readily. Sometimes, however, dogs will confuse the memory and diversion bird initially, but with practice they usually sort it out.

Alternate between throwing birds to first and second, third and second, and third and first. We suggest that for a while you always throw to second base as a diversion bird given that in our experience "back" tends to be a tougher command for dogs to master than "over."

Now that you have him retrieving double marked retrieves well, he is ready for triple marked retrieves in combination with hand signals. Take the same approach as you did earlier. Throw a dummy to first base, then one to third base, and finally toss one over his head to second base. Send him for retrieves first using the "back" command to the diversion bird, and then to memory dummies on either first or third base using the "over" command. Practice these diligently for a couple of weeks until you can rotate around the bases alternating between first, second, and third base as the diversion bird. When he is fully trained in basic baseball, you should be able to throw a memory bird to second base, a memory bird to first base, and a diversion bird to third base and have him retrieve in the order you indicate using a combination of voice and hand signals.

You are well on the way to having a hotshot retriever, and it is now time to move from the basics to a more advanced game of baseball. With this drill, you will put together all of the retrieving experience your canine friend has mastered so far and set the stage for a high degree of performance on hunt deads and blind retrieves, essentially retrieves where the dog does not see the bird fall to the ground. In advanced baseball, you want to expand the distances for each retrieve and add a little spice to challenge the dog's ability to follow your commands. Develop a drill that is comfortable for you to remember using the baseball diamond as point of reference. For example throw one dummy to third base while you are at home, and then throw a dummy to second base. Reposition yourself before sending the dog on a retrieve so you are in line with third, the mound, and first base but you are standing in the grand stands. Give the dog a right "over" and send him to second base. When he delivers the dummy to you, reposition him on first base and send him out using the "back" command for a long retrieve to third base. Using the pattern one dummy to the left and one over his head, move around the baseball field. The first retrieve is always a right "over" command while the second is always a long "back" command. You need to reposition yourself and the dog each time he makes a retrieve so that you move around the baseball field in a counterclockwise fashion. After working clockwise around the field, switch directions and go counterclockwise to practice left "overs." This drill varies the distance of the retrieves and also positions the dog so that he will have to make retrieves based upon your hand signals with the wind hitting him from various directions. The variations of baseball are limited only by your imagination. Moving to this level will not happen after two or three weeks of effort. If you start with the drills we outlined at the beginning of this section, it will take *several months, not weeks,* for your dog to be trained to handle the various retrieving situations we have discussed here. Once you make it to the advanced baseball stage, you are ready to move on to hunt deads and blind retrieves.

HUNT DEADS AND BLIND RETRIEVES: Hunt deads and blind retrieves are field skills that every good gun dog should be trained to perform. It is essential for the conservation of game, whether for hunting or to pass the hunt tests outlined in Chapter 8, for your dog to be capable of performing both of these types of retrieves. Essentially, the distinction between a blind retrieve and hunt dead rests upon the hunter's (or handler's as the case may be) *exact awareness* of where a bird fell. In a *blind retrieve*, the hunter knows exactly where in the field the bird fell after being shot, but the dog did not mark the fall. The hunter is able to handle a dog to the exact area of the fall using the commands "back" or "over." In a hunt test situation, the handler obviously did not shoot the bird, so that the position for the bird's fall is marked by his knowledge of where the bird might be and a judge's indication of a general area. The handler works to direct the dog to that spot to make the retrieve.

In a *hunt dead*, on the other hand, the hunter or handler has only an approximate idea where a bird might have fallen. In hunting, this can occur when a bird, wounded in flight, disappears over a grove of trees. The hunter notices the bird is falling, but is unable to pinpoint the bird's exact point of impact. In this instance, the hunter can only give a general line to the dog, coupled with a command to "hunt dead." In hunt deads, dogs do not take a specific line of direction, but will follow a general line to the targeted area and hunt in that direction. The drills we covered in the previous section are excellent for initially training your dog to perform both blind retrieves and hunt deads. In essence, whenever you gave him only a line of direction to an unmarked pile of dummies that he did not see you place on the ground, this was a blind retrieve. The drills he performed in baseball gave you the ability to further direct him to the fall of a dummy.

As in many, many things with gun dogs, the dog's *trust in the handler* is the single most important ingredient to blinds or hunt deads. The dog must be totally convinced that there is a bird or dummy to be retrieved when you give the "hunt dead" or "back" commands. That places a particular onus on the trainer to ensure that there is something for the dog to retrieve when the dog is given those commands. If the dog does not trust the handler, it will either quit its search for the downed bird or will not respond to your handling commands. Having discussed the training for blind retrieves extensively in the previous section, we will concentrate on training for hunt deads here.

Hunt dead training may start as soon as the puppy is retrieving well. For this drill you may use dummies, frozen birds, or freshly shot pigeons and you will also need to take his crate out to your training area. One approach is to crate the puppy and position the crate so that the puppy cannot see what you are doing. Take your dummy or bird and plant it in the grass, preferably under cover, no more than about five yards from your position. Alternatively you may leash your dog after you have performed some playground quartering drills in a ball field and start walking with the dog on lead back to the car or home. Carry a dummy casually in the opposite hand behind your back so the dog does not see the dummy. Nonchalantly, drop the dummy behind you, making certain your dog does not see you, and walk about three to five steps. Although these distances are very small initially, you will increase that distance after the dog understands what is expected of him and after he gains confidence.

Set up your first few hunt dead training sessions so the dog will run into the wind to make easier his task of finding the dummy. Often we have found a dog will even gain the scent of the object before you release him–this is thoroughly acceptable in the beginning stages of hunt dead training. Once the dummy or bird is planted, give him a while at "heel" and align your hand with his head, as if you were giving him a line. Use your hand to guide the dog's head in the direction you wish him to go. This is critical, because the dog will go in the direction his head is pointing. Give him "hunt dead" as the release command. If this is the first time you have used the "dead bird" or "back" (your choice, just be constant with the usage) command, no doubt your dog will give you that quizzical look that you have come to appreciate that implies one of you (not him) must have taken leave of their senses. Encourage him, and he will go a short distance, uncertain of what to do, until he hits that wall of scent that indicates that there is a dummy or bird.

When you feel your dog is responding well and finding the dummy short distances from you and have practiced the hunt dead drill using different wind directions, up the distance first to ten and later twenty yards. As the distances increase, you will need to incorporate the handling techniques of "back" and "over" to direct your dog to the area of the fall. If you are consistent in performing these drills and incorporate hunt dead training in your normal regime, you will find that your dog will develop a solid hunt dead capability and a high degree of trust in you.

STEADYING TO FLUSH AND SHOT: We train all of our gun dogs to be steady to flush and shot for a variety of reasons. Peace of mind is perhaps the most important reason, because you will not have to worry about your faithful friend chasing flushed birds over two counties after a hen flush or missed grouse. If you want your dog to participate in field trials, he must be steady to flush and shot or not be eligible for entry. Similarly, if hunt tests are your primary interest, beyond the beginner and immediate levels in most of the tests, dogs must be steady to flush and shot. Safety of the dog is also a primary consideration. In a hunting situation with a low flying bird, you do not want to run the risk of your dog being accidentally injured from being too close to the flushing bird when it is shot. Perhaps one of the most compelling arguments for steadying a dog is that it *downright looks good* and demonstrates to your friends and colleagues that the dog is hunting in control and is a "proper spaniel" in British terms.

There is, however, a school of thought that holds steadying does not help with game conservation, and the argument sounds something like this, "I don't want my dog steady, because I want him on that bird as soon as it hits the ground. That way I won't lose any cripples." It has been our experience, however, one loses no more game with a steady dog than an unsteady one. In fact, it appears to us that the opposite is true. Because when steady to flush and shot, the dog is forced to mark better by focusing on that spot where the bird lands. Better marking, we have found, results in more pinpoint retrieves and fewer hunt dead scenarios–especially when double marked retrieves are a concern. We readily admit steadying a dog to flush and shot perhaps is not for everyone or for every dog. Some dogs simply just do not want to be steady. If a dog refuses, despite the trainers best efforts to be steady, it may preclude some advanced hunt test work or field trial fun and games, but it really should not affect the dog's ability to hunt.

Steadying to flush and shot requires three essential ingredients–time, dedication, and money. Because it is a time-consuming endeav-

Locke Ridge KC JH WDX: A steady flush and shot dog -- the final product.
(Photo by Tony Roettger).

or, carefully pick the time that you wish to begin the steadying process. If you want to be hunting at the beginning of September, do not wait until mid-August to start steadying your hunting buddy. Similarly, do not wait until three weeks before that special field trial you have been targeting to start the process. Plan on spending a significant amount of time in the spring and summer months to get the job done prior to the fall hunting, field trial, and hunt test seasons.

We have also found that training your dog to be steady to flush and shot is often easier than maintaining this skill. Tough choices face you if, for example, you find yourself in South Dakota on that dream pheasant hunt on a crisp fall morning searching for that cock pheasant with a thirty inch tail for the wall in the den when your well trained steady to flush dog flushes that once-in-a-lifetime-bird, but the dog decides this is going to be the bird he breaks on. What do you do–shoot the bird and reward the dog for chasing it, or do you take the high road, allow the bird to escape, and apply immediate correction to the dog? This is a rough decision that cuts to the core of steady to flush and shot. You can shoot it but you just taught your dog that it is acceptable to break. Steadying is one of those absolutes if you give the dog an inch, he will take a mile. It cannot be selectively applied. It is confusing and unfair to the dog to resteady them after every hunting season.

You have already introduced your dog to both line steadiness and the quartering "hup." Initial steadiness training will build upon these two drills, so it is extremely important to have them down pat. Take the dog to your park, playground, or common area. Put a couple of dummies in your pocket and start the dog quartering as usual. As the dog is making a pass in the pattern throw a dummy behind you then hit the "hup" whistle. If he does not break, hold him in the "hup" very briefly and then call his name to release him for the retrieve. Clap yourself on the back several times vigorously and uncork the champagne for doing such a superlative job of preparing the dog.

What is far more likely, however, is he will make a move to retrieve the dummy. By throwing the dummy behind you, as you did in line steadying, you will be able to prevent the hard charging canine from making the retrieve should he break. If he does break, jump in front of the dog or physically grab him to ensure that he does not complete the retrieve using a firm yet happy demeanor. As soon as you have stopped his retrieve, "hup" him and then release the dog quickly by calling his name to make the retrieve. Do not wait a long time at this point for the retrieve. What is important right now is to stop him from chasing the dummy until released to make the retrieve. Once you release the dog to make the retrieve, chances are that he is confused and has lost his mark of the dummy's fall. Let him solve the problem and make the retrieve. Make a fuss over him for a good job. Repeat this exercise several times during the training session. A few evenings of this and the dog should be somewhat steady (or "honest" in the field trialer's jargon) on thrown dummies while quartering. It is important, however, that you *never let him make a retrieve when he breaks*. If uncertain, always place yourself in a position to prevent the dog from retrieving the dummy should he ever break. Be prepared to run him down to stop him from making the retrieve. Remember a retrieve is a dog's reward, not his right.

After you feel confident the dog will not break when you throw the dummy behind you, start throwing a dummy to either side of the dog. Progress to throwing them out in front of the dog after he has mastered the side throws. You will know that it is time to advance to the next stage when the dog "hups" a thrown dummy automatically and is not dependant upon hearing you blow a pip on the whistle (however, continue to blow the whistle). He is now "steady to thrown" in the jargon of dog trainers.

Once you have been training on thrown dummies for a while, the dog will begin to "pop." Popping is when the dog is constantly looking at you in anticipation of your throw of the dummy instead of running a quartering pattern searching for scent or hunting. When this starts to happen, and it will, keep the dog's mind on the quartering and the ground in front of him by planting a couple of dummies or dead birds in the field, field in advance of taking your dog to the quartering field, alternating sides a bit so he has to cover both sides of the field. This forces the dog to hunt and not constantly look back at you for the dummy throw. Mix in a few thrown dummies to keep things interesting.

To keep your dog on his paws, start preparing him for the fact that he will not get each retrieve. Every so often, throw a dummy, make certain that he "hups" as usual, and give him the "gone away" command to call him off the retrieve. This command is particularly useful if you plan to participate in field trials or hunt with a partner who also has a dog. Field trial rules require dogs running in braces (two dogs running on parallel courses) to "honor" the retrieve or flush of the dog on the other course by "hupping" and waiting for the other dog to complete its retrieve of a shot bird. When hunting with a partner whose dog is poised to retrieve a bird the dog flushed and the master shot, it is in very poor taste to have your dog swoop in for the retrieve.

In any case, you are seeking to have the dog ignore the thrown dummy and come back to you or commence hunting in a different direction that you indicate. You have the option to pick that dummy up immediately, quarter the dog a little way down the field and send him back for the dummy as a blind retrieve, or leave the dummy in the field and use it later on for hunt dead practice. Mix it up a bit to keep the dog guessing. In the beginning stages of this training he will naturally want to make this retrieve, do not allow him to. Give the "no" or "ahhh" command in a firm tone and repeat "gone away" and a few pips on the whistle. This will make him a very solid, steady dog in the future.

Once you have mastered the dummies, advance to using dead birds, clipped-wing pigeons, and eventually to thrown pigeons. If you have access to a homing pigeon flock through a local flushing dog hunting club or professional trainer, use them in this stage of training; they are worth the squab's weight in gold as they can be reused many times. Continue to use dead birds and clipped-wing pigeons even if you have access to homing pigeons to keep the flush strong as well as to keep the dog hunting. One cautionary note here is you probably will want to conduct this training in wildlife management areas, on hunt club grounds, during local dog club training days, or at nearby professional training facilities so as not to offend the tender sensibilities of some of the people who frequent playgrounds or commons areas. Use common sense when employing live or dead birds as training aids.

It is now time to put it all together and complete the steadying process. Plan a quartering course carefully, and make certain that you plant a flight capable pigeon so the dog will be able to flush the bird. Use strong flight worthy birds so that they will flush hard and fly when the dog makes a leap to catch the pigeon. Our suggestion would be to plant it as you are quartering the dog, not in advance, even if the dog is able to see you plant the bird. In a perfect world the dog will "hup" when the bird flies off and you hit the whistle. The primary handler mistake made at this point in the steadying process is to blow the whistle *far too early into the flush*. *Do not blow the whistle* until the bird has flushed and flown completely out of the dog's reach. Timing is extremely critical at this junction. Should you blow the whistle to call for the "hup" too soon, you risk turning your flushing dog into a pointing dog, instead of obtaining a solid performing spaniel or retriever that is steady to flush and shot.

If at this point the dog does not "hup" to a flushed and flying pigeon, you must take your whistle out of your mouth and not say another word. Go retrieve the dog, again without saying a word, and shake him up a bit as you carry him back to the exact location where he broke. Place the dog down and give the "hup" command via whistle and voice then let him sit there for a few moments. Repeat the exercise until he gets it absolutely right. Remember, patience, do not loose your temper, and recognize that dogs are different and learn at different rates. You may have to experiment with the process a little to determine exactly what will work with your particular dog. In the end, however, you will have a superbly trained dog that is rock-steady on flushed birds–a source of pride for you both. When using live flyers, keep a clipped-wing or dead pigeon in your vest pocket. When he stops on the flyer–throw the dead bird to give him a "reward." When you are ready to actually shoot the bird, remember to wait until the dog stops after the flush before you shoot it. Many dogs will begin by breaking on the shot so you need to be prepared for this potential development. All of this is made much easier when you have a friend with you to help.

WIND AND PATTERNING: The ability to utilize the wind and adjust your dog's patterning in the field is difficult to teach and something that comes with handling experience. The wind and how one's dog uses it effectively to find and flush game can be quite confusing. Seasoned field trialers in many cases disagree about what the optimum pattern is, given certain wind conditions. The best advice we can offer is essentially to trust in your dog's innate ability to use the wind optimally to locate game. Most dogs will pattern very naturally and use the wind to best advantage. Some pattern correctly, but get caught up in too big of a down wind loops, thus hunting out of effective gun range. The key is to find a balance between your dog's use of the wind to locate birds, and staying within the range of your shotgun.

English springer spaniel Jake McGee SH flushes a rooster; owner John Pidde. (Photo by Tony Roettger).

SEVEN

The Professional: Asking For Help and Making it Worthwhile

No matter how diligently you train your gun dog, sooner or later you probably will seek the help of a professional to iron out those little wrinkles you have either because of the lack the time, expertise, or both to correct. This is especially true if you seek to run your dog in field trials, wish to progress beyond the Junior Hunter title in hunt tests, or are interested in having a truly polished field performer. We have found that most of the dogs whelped at or procured abroad by Roettger Ridge Kennels and subsequently sold to customers who live in cities, return to the kennel usually several times for focused training. Many of those who send their dogs back to Roettger Ridge are seeking advanced gun dog training-- such as steadying to wing and shot, advanced bird work, or other training that cannot for whatever reason be accomplished in the city. These clients recognize that there is a limit to what they can achieve without professional training facilities and a heavy dose of game birds.

Often gun dog owners seek professional help to overcome a specific problem that is defying the owner's attempts to solve. For example, if a dog exhibits a case of hard mouth or excessive chewing of birds or dummies, refuses to retrieve, retrieves but fails to deliver to hand, or fails to heed calls to return on "gone aways," a professional can generally help to mitigate or eliminate those tendencies. What a professional cannot do is *turn a sow's ear into a silk purse.* By this we mean that just like the owner, a professional trainer needs solid material with which to work.

Perhaps more than anything else, what a really good professional does is to train the amateur trainer–assuming of course that the amateur is "trainable." It takes a rare breed of professional to recognize that he or she is as much of a psychologist as an animal behaviorialist. Almost all faults associated with gun dogs have their root causes in something an inexperienced trainer did during some part of the training process–gun shyness, poor obedience, poor retrieves–you name it, and some amateur along the way has probably botched it. It is likely the professional's single greatest contribution is to erect a solid foundation for trainer and dog alike that will enable a hard working, savvy amateur to build upon in training a successful gun dog.

SELECTING THE RIGHT PROFESSIONAL: If you were able to select your breeder and a professional trainer at the same time you purchased your dog along the lines we indicated in the first chapter, you may wish to skip this section. However, we have found often an owner, having purchased a dog from a kennel specializing in gun dogs, may seek a different professional as a trainer. This may occur because the breeding kennel is too far removed from the owner's city of residence; the breeder may not be heavily into training; or the owner simply is interested in a fresh approach. Whatever the reasons, if you are seeking a professional trainer, there are many paths to finding the one must suitable to your needs. All roads to the professional, however, start with research.

One of the best methods a dog owner can use to link up with the right pro is to visit hunt tests, field trials, or participate in local gun dog club training days and talk to successful handlers who have had their dogs professionally trained. The following should help you in the selection process:

✦ **Evaluate other amateur handlers and dogs:** Seek out the best performing dogs and handlers at the event. Ask yourself these questions: does the dog act skittish, hesitant, or tentative when performing field tasks? How do the handler and dog interact? Are they close; is a relationship based upon mutual affection? What methods does he or she use to control the dog? Are the words or actions harsh? Watching dogs and their handlers may tell you a little about the professional and his or her training techniques. It does, however, tell you if you wish to rely upon a handler's recommendation.

✦ **Study Trade Periodicals and Web Sites:** *Gun Dog Magazine, The Retriever Journal, Spaniels in the Field, Shooting Sportsman*, and *Sporting Classics, Gray's Sporting Journal,* and *The Upland Almanac* all carry articles on gun dogs, training techniques, and professional trainers. Similarly, online magazines and breed associations give excellent leads on professionals. The English Springer Spaniel Field Trial Association (www.essfta.org), the English Cocker Spaniel Club of America (www.eesea.org), *Gun Dogs Online Magazine* (www.gundogsonline.com), *The Spaniel Journal* (www.spanieljournal.com), The *English Springer Spaniel Information and Field Trial* web site (www.essft. com), *Bird Dog & Retriever News* web site (www.bird-dog-news.com), and the *Cockers in the Field* web site (www. fieldcockers.com) also provide articles, breeder information, and leads on professional trainers.

✦ **Interviews:** Make a list of those professional trainers you believe will be compatible with your style of training and philosophy. This is one of the toughest things to do. We suggest that you start with a list of ten or so professionals. If you have taken our advice and visited some hunt tests or field trials, joined a hunting spaniel or retriever club, and participated in club training days, you will have made some solid contacts in the gun dog world. Have someone with whom you feel comfortable who is also knowledgeable about professional trainers evaluate your list to help you reduce the numbers. If you have not been able to visit a hunt test or field trial and have not joined a club, your list will be a little larger.

✦ **Visits and references:** If at all possible, we encourage you to visit the kennel to inspect first hand the training and kennel facilities and discuss your requirements face to face with the professional. If you visit, closely observe the set up. The facilities should be reasonably clean. We say *reasonably* because the gun dog training business inherently involves a degree of mess. The most important element is that the facilities *offer a healthy living and working environment and the dogs appear well kept.* This is not often as straightforward as it seems.

Several years ago, a woman in search of a suitable professional related a horror story to us. She had been visiting various kennels not far from her home when she came upon one in a particularly ramshackle facility with crates of dogs stored haphazardly in various sheds and outbuildings. One building housed a couple of dogs in what appeared to be on the surface an acceptable kennel run with fresh sawdust covering the run area. Upon closer inspection, she noticed that the dogs were up to their chests in sawdust indicating that they actually were standing in accumulated piles of their own filth. If you cannot get recommendations from people you know and trust and cannot visit the facility, make certain you get references from the professional before you send your dog to their facilities. Should a professional be reluctant to give you references, consider it a red flag.

Normally you are able to readily obtain email addresses and telephone numbers from advertisements or references. Draft an email of your objectives for training your dog. Try to be as precise as you can, and send it *individually* (you do not want to appear is if you are shopping for the lowest competitive mortgage rate rather than a hunting companion) to the professionals on your list. Follow the email up with telephone interviews with those responding to your email. Ask the tough questions about training techniques, costs, electric collar use, trained retrieve techniques, etc. It is important to understand each professional's approach and philosophy of training.

If you have been diligent in your background research and meticulous in your interviews of professional trainers, you will be ready to make your choice. Make certain that you clearly understand what is involved in having a professional train your dog. When you find a professional that meets your requirements, is patient, and willing to teach not only your dog, but you as well, you will have gone a long way toward making the training experience a rewarding one. Relinquishing one's dog to another person for training is an important and potentially emotional experience; it is not always an easy thing to do. Most gun dog owners feel a strong sense of personal attachment to their dogs. There are many good professional trainers who have dedicated their lives to developing the best gun dogs available today. The trick is to find one compatible with your needs and personal style and one you feel you can trust.

SET AND MANAGE MUTUAL EXPECTATIONS: Before you seek professional advice, carefully evaluate *what* you want the professional to accomplish for you and write it down before you discuss it with the trainer over the phone. If, for example, you are seeking help with steadying your dog to flush and shot, overcoming basic retrieving issues, control during field situations, instilling the trained retrieve, work on blinds, or any of the other countless gun dog training tasks professionals are routinely called upon to perform, it is essential that you and the professional have a clear understanding as to what is involved. Questions such as how long will the training take, what specifically is involved in the training, kennel facilities, what needs to be done to prepare the dog for training, the cost for the training, transportation to and from the professional's location, veterinarian and health issues all need to be discussed prior to commencing the training.

Professionals routinely are asked to take dogs with little or no field breeding and turn them into a highly trained gun dog. Many owners expect that a professional, given any kind of spaniel or retriever, can produce a dog that can pass the Senior or Master Hunter level in hunt tests, perform flawlessly in the field, live harmoniously with a family at home, and bring home the blue ribbons in the show ring. Although a very laudable ideal for a dog owner who seeks an all-around dog, it is exceedingly difficult for even professional trainers to achieve. It will certainly cost an arm, leg, and perhaps a first-born child to achieve. A good professional will lead the novice through the minefields of expectations versus reality and the best ones will preempt your questions. After all, a professional has as much at stake as you do–mainly the professional's reputation. Therefore, it is as much in the professional's interest to have clear expectations as it is in yours.

LAY THE GROUNDWORK FOR PROFESSIONAL TRAINING: To dramatically increase your chances of success, work with your professional well in advance to identify drills you can do at home to prepare your dog as much as possible for the professional. A professional will obtain far quicker results for you, if he or she can concentrate on those tasks that are difficult for the urban dweller to accomplish. Most professionals prefer to spend their time putting the finishing touches on dogs, rather than have to deal with elementary training such as housebreaking, beginning retriever work, or obedience. Unless the dog owner is having significant problems in one of the basic training areas, it is much better to accomplish basic dog training prior to sending the dog to the pro. Unfortunately, this is one of the areas amateurs and novices most often overlook–probably because of a lack of dialog with the professional. Failure to prepare your dog for the professional can lead to some nasty surprises on both ends and specifically to significantly increased training costs.

There is much the urban gun dog owner can do to prepare the dog for the professional. For example, if you want the pro to steady your dog to flush and shot, prepare your dog by line steadying him to thrown dummies. A line steady dog generally is much easier to steady to flush and shot, than a non-line steady dog. A dog that is line steady will, in all likelihood, require far fewer birds and less professional time than one who is not. This translates into distinct cost-savings for the owner. If you are seeking greater control over your dog in the field, do basic obedience and quartering drills in your common or park area. The key is to drill in as much control as possible prior to turning the dog over to the professional. *The more the urban gun dog owner can accomplish in training prior to sending the dog to the professional, the more effective and cheaper the training.*

CONSIDER ADDITIONAL TRAINING FOR YOURSELF: No professional training is going to be effective if the dog owner does not dedicate time to follow it up with the right kind of training. This usually encompasses the two objects of training: the dog and the owner. It is fairly easy for the urban gun dog owner to pack the dog up and send him off to the professional. It is far more difficult for the owner to break away and join the dog at some point during the training. For a novice trainer, spending time with a professional who has been or is training the novice's dog is invaluable. Learning a task the correct way the first time is far easier than unlearning an ingrained habit. Roettger Ridge takes in dogs from owners who live all over the United States for all manner of training. It is a rare owner, aside from those living within reasonable driving distances who frequents the kennel on the weekends, that visits North Branch, Minnesota to sharpen his or her skills after the dog completes his training. An urban gun dog owner should seriously consider spending a day or two with the professional trainer with his or her dog to pick up nuances pertaining to the dog, to learn handling tips, and to understand how better to re-enforce the dog's training. Look upon this as a mini-vacation to train and relax with friends. If planned for, it can help the owner capitalize on a sound investment in the dog.

Not long ago, a professional gun dog trainer and colleague received an inquiry concerning professional training for his young eighteen-month old English cocker that would center specifically on control issues. Evidently the owner took him to the park to play and found that he had "strong retrieving and bird finding skills" and wanted our friend to work with him. Digging deeper into the details, the professional trainer discovered that the owner would routinely encourage the dog to chase geese as they loitered around the park's pond. The agitated geese would run *pall mall* into the street followed by the wild-eyed cocker unless stopped by the owner, thereby creating a dangerous situation for man and beast. The real issue here was not so much dog control problems, but *owner handling problems*. Novice handlers are often at a loss as to how to control dogs due to their own lack of experience. This owner and the dog ultimately benefited significantly from regular training. Today the owner is an experienced handler and owns a well-trained, finely tuned gun dog that is as comfortable living in the city as he is hunting pheasant and grouse.

PRO RAPPORT: It is extremely important to develop a solid relationship with your professional of choice. The best of all possible worlds is if you view him or her as a combination of mentor, coach, and friend. After all, the primary reason you have chosen to place your developing national champion in a professional's tender loving care, is because a professional trainer can accomplish things you, through of lack of experience or facilities, cannot. It should go without saying an owner, having adhered to the scrupulous professional selection process, should actually take the professional's advice. Unfortunately this is not always the case. Professionals deal with a wide variety of owners–some are rank novices, but many have extensive experience. Pros routinely handle a large number of dogs, generally have a significant amount of experience handling dogs for hunt tests and field trials, and are often themselves highly accomplished judges for field trials and hunt tests. For example, if you plan to run your dog in hunt tests or field trials and you are going to be handling the dog yourself, it is a good idea to let the professional watch you handle the dog. Be prepared for some constructive criticism and consider it carefully.

In short, the professional's experience base tends to be much, much higher than the average amateur. After all, no matter how much you learn in gun dog training and handling, there is always something new a wise person can learn.

Find a good professional and stay with him or her. Often we see owners, especially those involved in the highly competitive world of field trials, send a dog to one professional for training and have the dog handled in competition by a different professional. To be frank, this is a head-scratcher. It seems to us both counter-intuitive and counter-productive to change horses in the middle of a stream. A dog develops a rapport with a professional during training and, unless that professional is cruel or brutal (this is exceedingly rare), learns to respond to the trainer. It takes time and effort for a dog to become adjusted to a new handler who is not the owner. Often much is lost in the transition between the two. Our advice is to find a good professional and stay the course.

After a professional has worked with your dog, give the dog a chance to become conditioned to your particular handling style. Often what appears to be a problem resolves itself after a dog becomes adjusted to its owner's handling technique. Routinely we will see dogs that have been professionally trained revert to old habits when they return home. This happens quite often where dogs have been under a professional's care for several months.

Not long ago, Roettger Ridge had a dog in for steadying to flush and shot and other advanced training. This particular dog spent six months at the kennel preparing for what would be an exhaustive field trial season. Several days after the dog returned home, the owner called extremely concerned that the dog had made little or no progress. The owner was told to work with the dog for a week or two to give the dog some time to make the transition from one handler to the other. Several weeks later the owner called to say that the dog was performing superbly. Sometimes, it just takes a little time and patience after a dog is professionally trained for the dog to get in synch again with your handling style.

A second example is equally illuminating. Several years ago, a hunter with substantial experience hunting with flushing dogs, but who had never owned a "finished" gun dog sent his young spaniel to the kennel for steadying to flush and shot well in advance of a South Dakota pheasant hunt. Shortly before departing for the trip, the owner picked up the dog and had a session or two at the kennel before his trip began. The dog was as steady as the rock of Gibraltar.

While in South Dakota, they hunted fencerows, which are very narrow and tend to concentrate birds into a small section, and are very difficult for a young inexperienced dog to hunt. Pheasants like to run and when faced with a determined hunter and well-trained dog, the smarter ones (they live longer) tend to run away from the hunter and canine predators. The kennel received a late night call from a panic stricken owner. The dog took all these running birds well, flushed them and even remained steady. However, the owner was concerned because the dog was not quartering properly; the dog. it seems, was running straight down the fence line until it flushed a bird. Given that the grass on the fences was scarcely more than a yard or two wide, there was precious little for dog to quarter in. After assimilating all the facts of the case, the professional suggested the handler try some open prairie grassland the next day to give the dog something in which to quarter. The result was a full game bag and a happy owner. This particular issue was resolved successfully because the owner and the professional had developed a strong rapport and were able to sort the problem out quickly. It was a field handling issue stemming from the relative inexperience of this particular hunter in working with a very steady dog.

RE-ENFORCE THE TRAINING: Irrespective of whether or not an urban gun dog owner can spend some quality time with the professional while the dog is in training, it is absolutely critical the owner develop in cooperation with the professional a plan to re-enforce the dog's training. For example, a dog that has recently been steadied to flush and shot requires re-enforcement or will quickly regress. To re-enforce this training, you probably will want to spend a little time at a local game preserve. The last thing you want, especially if your dog competes in field trials or hunt tests, is to discover belatedly that for some reason he has "forgotten" those professional lessons. Similarly, if your dog has had extensive retriever training on birds, you will have to develop a plan to keep the training fresh in the dog's mind. Exercise the contacts in the gun dog world you have made. Find out where you can get birds with which to train. Make a plan to go to a wildlife management area on the weekend to train with a friend. After having spent the time, effort, and money to have a dog trained by a professional, the urban gun dog owner must ensure that dog does not slip back into old habits. A training re-enforcement plan is critical to ensure continued progress.

EIGHT

Hunt Tests, Field Trials, and Handling for the Field

By this time you are probably irrevocably hooked on your dog and his training. No doubt you have bored your spouse to tears talking about the intricate and technical details of gun dog training. All of your non-hunting friends now run when they see you coming, convinced that you are about to button-hole them and start showing the most recent pictures of your canine pride and joy for the fourth time. It is abundantly clear you have the gun dog bug and have it badly. You subscribe to the gun dog periodicals; your coffee cup, necktie, blouse, skirt, or shirt sport insignias of your dog's breed. You are now prepared to move to a higher plane.

For the city dwelling gun dog owner, handler, and trainer, hunt tests, field trials, and plain old hunting offer strong incentives to devote the time and effort to training your flushing dog. These activities are the core around which gun dog clubs form. As such, they bring you together with people who share your interest and can assist you in training and developing both your skills and that of your dog.

Three organizations in the United States sponsor hunt or field tests and grant titles that appear either before or after the dog's name. The beauty of a hunt test is, unlike highly competitive field trials, neither the handler nor the dog competes against another handler/dog team.

Instead, the handler and the dog are measured against a standard. It is an ideal way for novice and experienced handlers alike to sharpen the skills of handler and dog. All three organizations have developed standards a dog must meet prior to gaining the title. There are some significant differences between the standards each organization has established, but there are very common threads running through all of the standards associated with training all hunting dogs must have. These hunting tests are great fun. They offer a camaraderie not typically found in field trials, a highly competitive sport, and offer a unique opportunity for the handlers at all levels to meet, exchange ideas, and test their skills as trainers and handlers against a common foe–the judges. Each of the three sponsoring organizations host clubs for dog enthusiasts that offer the opportunity to train, sponsor hunting-style tests, and promote the sport. Many clubs seek multiple sponsorships under one or more of the parent organizations, so as to increase the opportunities for their members to participate in hunting-style tests.

AKC hunt tests are open to AKC registered dogs within their individual category (authors' note: the retriever owner may wish to skip the section on AKC spaniel hunt tests, spaniel field trials, spaniel breed association certificate programs, and hunt test and field trial handling, and concentrate on the United Kennel Club and North American Hunting Retriever Association sections). For example, AKC flushing spaniel hunt test eligibility includes: English springer spaniels, English cocker spaniels, American cocker spaniels, Sussex spaniels, Clumber spaniels, and field spaniels–essentially those spaniel breeds the AKC recognizes for conformation events. Retrievers and pointers have their own hunt test standards distinct from spaniels. The North American Hunting Retriever Association takes a slightly different approach. NAHRA field tests are open to all AKC registered retrievers, and as of December 2003 now allows all AKC registered spaniel breeds to participate in the full range of NAHRA hunt tests (called field tests in the NAHRA lexicon). The United Kennel Club (UKC) offers its own version of the hunt test and is open to all spaniel and retriever breeds that UKC officially recognizes. The UKC requires dogs to be registered with the organization in order to earn titles.

AKC hunt tests for spaniels are designed to simulate the upland game-hunting scenario a hunter would encounter in pheasant, grouse, or quail hunting. Their purpose is to measure game finding, flushing, and retrieving abilities in a variety of upland game situations. On the other hand, the UKC and NAHRA emphasize the retrieving aspects of hunting most commonly associated with waterfowl and dove shooting. These tests involve simulating a variety of retrieving scenarios designed to test a dog's ability to retrieve marked and unmarked retrieves on land and water. Nothing precludes a spaniel owner with a dog that is eligible to participate in both styles of hunt test from doing so. However, we should point out that the training regimes and techniques are quite different for the two styles of hunt test. Hunt tests are sponsored by individual sporting dog clubs. A good way to get into hunt tests is to join a club that is in the area. The AKC, UKC, NAHRA, and individual breed associations all maintain lists of clubs nationwide that cater to the spaniel and retriever breeds. Often the club's major annual event will be the hunt test or field trial. These clubs also offer training days for handlers and dogs in advance of a hunt test to help the city-bound handler tune up for a test.

AMERICAN KENNEL CLUB HUNT TESTS: The AKC divides its hunt test titles into Junior Hunter, Senior Hunter, and Master Hunter categories that require dogs to pass increasingly demanding tests governed by a set of standards for each level. The standards, in turn, are reflected in a series of test situations designed to simulate conditions a hunter would encounter during a hunt. A dog striving for a Junior Hunter title must demonstrate the basic hunting skills of bird finding in a variety of different cover situations, must be enthusiastic, hunt within range of the guns, be capable of basic quartering, and able to retrieve shot birds to a close proximity of the handler (usually measured as a couple of big steps). A Junior Hunter dog does not have to be steady to flush and shot, but should hunt under control. The dog must handle reasonably well, defined as the handler not having to use excessive voice or whistle commands to control the dog, and not chase flyaway birds excessively.

The Junior Hunter tests consist of two phases—a land portion and a water retrieve. The land test is run on a course that is usually three

Two judges look on at this AKC hunt test while the handler prepares to run the land course. (Photo by John Durand).

to four hundred yards in length with a reasonable amount of cover. The handler and two judges stand in the middle of the course with two gunners deployed approximately fifteen yards to the left and right of the handler. Bird stewards plant birds at various points along the course for the dogs to find and flush. A Junior Hunter is required to flush and retrieve two birds to the handler, although the dog does not have to retrieve to "hand." Junior Hunter land tests usually, although not always, run the dogs directly into the wind to aid the young dogs in quartering and finding the birds. At the judge's signal, the handler sends his dog out to hunt. The dog should range back and forth between the guns on either side of the handler and no more than about ten yards in front of the handler. Once the dog finds and flushes the birds one of the two guns (sometimes both) will shoot the bird and the dog will then be expected to retrieve the shot bird (assuming the guns are reasonably good shots).

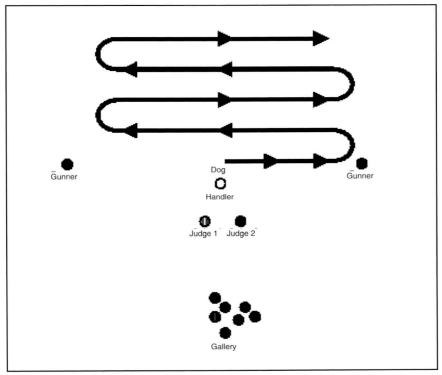

Diagram 5. Hunt Test Quartering Field

Judges score the Junior Hunter according to a scorecard system the AKC has developed. After all the dogs in the running order complete their land runs, the judges will invite or "call back" those dogs successfully completing the land portion of the test to the water test. The Junior Hunter water test consists of a single marked retrieve of a previously shot bird thrown approximately twenty yards from the handler and dog. The handler, dog, and judges stand at the bank of a pond prior to the bird being thrown. In the Junior Hunter category, the handler may lightly restrain the dog to keep it from breaking when the bird hits the water. Once the handler has the dog "hupped" and under control, the judge will signal the bird stewards to throw the bird. Generally a shot is fired from a blank gun or shotgun to simulate the shooting of the bird. Often bird stewards will sound a duck call prior to throwing the bird to gain the dog's attention. The judge will then tap the handler on the shoulder and he will release the dog for the retrieve that is relatively short, approximately twenty to thirty yards.

To obtain the Junior Hunter title, which appears as the suffix "JH" on the AKC official registration form, a dog must successfully pass this same test four times (they need not be consecutive). A successful passing of a test, called " a leg" in the hunt test lexicon, will result in the dog being awarded an orange AKC hunt test ribbon with a rosette. When the dog passes all four legs, the AKC sends out an award certificate.

The Senior Hunter test builds upon the foundation laid during training for Junior Hunter. Although, there is no AKC requirement to pass each level in turn from Junior Hunter to Senior Hunter then to Master Hunter, the standards assume a dog passing a Senior level hunt test would be fully capable of passing a Junior Hunter hunt test. If a dog has a Junior Hunter title, then it needs to pass four legs in order to get its Senior Hunter. If a dog seeks a Senior Hunter title without first gaining a Junior Hunter title, the dog must pass five legs of the Senior Hunter test. Once a leg has been earned at a higher level, the dog cannot be entered at the lower level.

The standards for Senior Hunter predictably are quite a bit stiffer than for Junior Hunter. There is the same land series and a water test, but at the Senior level, the standards require an additional land series called the "hunt dead" which is essentially a blind retrieve. As in Junior, the standards call for two retrieves of flushed and shot birds, but the judges are looking for a far more polished hunting style, greater handler control of the dog, and a retrieve to hand. The "hunt dead" land portion is a blind retrieve in cover of approximately thirty yards. To successfully pass the "hunt dead" the dog must be capable of taking a line and basic handling. To successfully pass the thirty-yard water retrieve, the dog must steady to shot and a thrown bird and may not be restrained by a leash or hand.

The AKC spaniel Master Hunter test is a significant jump for a dog from Senior Hunter. The Master Hunter standard requires absolute steadiness to flush and shot during the land test, a mastery of quartering in a variety of wind conditions and directions, superior bird finding ability, and polished retrieve to hand. The Master Hunter "hunt dead" is longer than the Senior Hunter version and requires superb handling, bird finding, and delivery skills. To pass the water retrieve, a dog must be rock steady and capable of a forty to fifty yard water retrieve.

Perhaps the most difficult portion of the spaniel AKC Master Hunter test, is the water blind. A dog must be able to take a line to a downed bird that forces the dog to swim thirty plus yards to the bird. Frequently, but not always, the bird is on the opposite bank. Once the dog finds the bird and makes the retrieve, he returns to the handler preferably by swimming back across the pond to the handler. However, dogs may "run the bank" back around the pond to the handler for a lower score. To gain a Master Hunter title a dog possessing a Senior Hunter title must pass five legs. Without a Senior Hunter, the standards require a dog to pass successfully six Master Hunter legs. There has been some discussion of developing a beyond the master level for AKC flushing spaniels, and there have been some prototype hunt tests run as a precursor to establishing standards for such a level. The English Springer Spaniel Field Trial Association, AKC parent club, has established a beyond the Master Hunter level certificate (see the section on *Breed Organization Working Dog and Working Dog Excellent Certificates),* but it likely will be years before the AKC adopts a similar title for spaniels.

NORTH AMERICAN HUNTING RETRIEVER ASSOCIATION FIELD TESTS: NAHRA field tests are more closely akin to AKC retriever hunt tests than spaniel hunt tests, and the organization confers four titles–Started Hunting Retriever (SR), Working Retriever (WR), Master Hunting Retriever (MHR), and Grand Master Hunting Retriever (GMHR). But for those addicted to the hunt test scene, NAHRA field tests offer a significant challenge to spaniel and retriever owners beyond the AKC's Master Hunter title and a wholly unique style of training. Until the AKC adopts the beyond the Master Hunter level title, NAHRA field test may offer the only available real challenge, aside from competitive field trials, to AKC registered spaniels and retrievers once a dog has achieved a Master Hunter title. And, they are really tough challenges, particularly for spaniels as they have as a breed not participated in the NAHRA program to the extent that the retriever breeds have. For a spaniel to attain the level of a Grand Master Hunting Retriever, would be quite a feat indeed given their temperament and strong hunting instinct.

The Started Hunting Retriever standard is not unlike that of the AKC Junior Hunter. NAHRA requires four successful passes of the SR field test–or the accumulation of 2.5 points per leg for a total of 10 points. The test consists of five single bird marking tests consisting of at least two marked water and two marked land retrieves. The fifth may be either a marked land or marked water retrieve at the judges' discretion. Similar to the Junior Hunter water retrieve, a Started Hunting Retriever must be steady at the point of origin, essentially where the dog marks the retrieve, but may be held steady using a leash or slip-lead. The land retrieves are not to exceed seventy-five yards and the water retrieves may not be longer than fifty yards. The dog must exhibit solid marking, and retrieving potential. Again like the AKC Junior Hunter standards, retrieves at this level do not have to be to hand.

The Working Retriever level, the NAHRA intermediate category, is a significant step up from the Started Hunting Retriever level. The test consists of five portions: an upland hunting test, a blind water retrieve, a double marked land retrieve, a double marked water retrieve, and a trailing test. Like the AKC Senior Hunter and Master Hunter water retrieves, dogs must steady at the point of origin and all retrieves must be to hand. Dogs may be handled using voice and whistle commands on both land and water. Land distances may not exceed one hundred yards for the double marked retrieves and distances are to be no more than seventy-five yards for the double marked water retrieves. The water blind is to be fifty yards or less. The point requirements for the Working Retriever level are a little different than that of the Started Hunting Retriever. Each successful leg earns the dog 5 points toward a 20-point requirement–again passing scores on four legs.

The senior testing level is the most demanding NAHRA level and corresponds to the Master Hunter level of the AKC. Again the test scenario is completely different. The NAHRA senior field test consists of six tests that include a triple marked land retrieve, a triple marked

This water retrieve resulted in Roettger Ridge's Andy JH earning his Junior Hunter title. (Photo by John Durand).

water retrieve, an upland hunting test (with flush), a water blind retrieve, a land blind retrieve, and a trailing test. Either the water blind or the land blind retrieves will be included in either the triple water marked retrieve or the triple land marked retrieve. The dogs must be steady to shot. The maximum test distances may not be greater than one hundred yards for all test events. Each qualifying leg nets a dog 20 points against a 100-point Master Hunting Retriever requirement. With a Working Retriever title, a dog need pass only four legs to gain the title.

Beyond the Master Hunting Retriever level, is the Grand Master Hunting Retriever title. There is no separate test for Grand Master Hunting Retriever. For a dog to attain the GMHR prefix, it must amass 300 points in senior field tests—a rough enough standard. At 20 points awarded per leg, a dog must pass the senior field test many times in order to receive the title—a level that may be totally beyond the capabilities of your run of the mill field-bred English springer spaniel.

NAHRA field test series offer difficult testing scenarios sufficient to raise goose bumps on the flesh of true "hunt test junkies." For those handlers truly dedicated to hunting and field tests, NAHRA might be a sound supplement to the AKC variety.

UNITED KENNEL CLUB HUNTS: And if the AKC and NAHRA hunt and field tests are not enough, The United Kennel Club, the second largest club in the United States after the AKC, also has its own variety of hunt test. The UKC hunt test is more like the NAHRA version and concentrates heavily on more traditional non-slip retriever style of test scenarios. As in the NAHRA program, spaniels and retrievers both ply their skills against a common standard. Dogs must be UKC-registered (within 60 days of passing a hunt) in order to receive credit for a pass, and nothing precludes a dog from being dual AKC-UKC registered. The UKC test program is open to all breeds of purebred spaniels and retrievers registered with the UKC. The UKC's program also differs from the AKC and NAHRA test in its point structure. Although the NAHRA program does have a point program, it essentially corresponds to the AKC passes or legs at each level. The program includes three primary testing levels, called "Hunts" in the UKC system–Started, Seasoned, and Finished levels–but titles are earned on the basis of points awarded for each of the different types of tests. There is a fourth level of Hunt only open to certain dogs called the Grand Hunt. In addition to the Hunts, there is a separate category of testing known as the Upland Hunt unrelated to the three retriever categories. After the Started Hunting Retriever level, there are several paths toward the various titles of Started Hunting Retriever (SHR), Hunting Retriever (HR), Hunting Retriever Champion (HRCH), Grand Hunting Retriever Champion (GRHRCH), and the additional Upland Hunter (UH) title. Although the UKC program starts out similar to AKC and NAHRA programs, it begins to diverge after the Started Retriever category.

The Started Retriever, the first level of the UKC hunting retriever program is similar to NAHRA's test at this level. The Started Retriever test consists of four marked single retrieves–two on land and two on water. The marked land retrieves are not to be longer than seventy-five yards, while the water retrieves may not exceed sixty yards.

Started dogs are held at a line, and at the Started Retriever level, dogs need not be steady–again very similar to the NAHRA standards. The UKC also awards points for the Started Hunting Retriever category. At the Started level, a dog may receive 5 points per successful pass of a UKC hunt toward its goal of 20 points required to receive the Started Hunting Retriever prefix. Judges will look for retrieving and hunting desire in dogs. At the Started Hunting Retriever level, only dead birds are used and they must be delivered to the immediate vicinity of the handler–a similar standard to that of the AKC Junior Hunter level and the NAHRA Started Retriever standard. Upon successful completion of the four legs, a dog is awarded the SHR prefix preceding the dog's name. After the relatively straightforward Started Hunt level, the UKC program gets a little more complex and there is an element of strategy involved as to how the handler approaches the various levels of hunt.

The Seasoned Hunt test level consists of five tests: a double marked land retrieve, a double marked water retrieve, a walkup, tracking, or quartering test, a land blind retrieve, and water blind retrieve. In addition, there must be a diversion bird in part of the test. The distances for the retrieves at this level are predictably longer than for the Started level. Land retrieves may not be longer than one hundred yards, water retrieves may not exceed seventy-five yards, and neither land nor water blinds may be longer than forty yards.

Dogs must be line steady at this level without restraint. However, the standards allow for a "controlled break" with substantial penalties, but not necessarily outright failure at the Seasoned level. A controlled break occurs when the dog is at the line and begins a retrieve without command from the handler. If the handler is quick on his toes and recalls the dog before the dog gets too far off the line, a controlled break has occurred. Retrieves must be to hand. A successful pass at the Season testing level results in the award of ten championship points with a total number of points a dog may earn at this level is limited to forty points unless the dog has previously earned ten points at the Started level. If the dog has Started points, he is allowed to earn a maximum of only thirty points at the Seasoned level.

The highest level of testing, the Finished Hunt test category, sets the bar even higher. A Finished Hunt has four tests: a multiple marked water retrieve, a multiple marked land retrieve, a water blind, and a land blind. Either or both the multiple water or land retrieves must include a diversion bird and an honor of a retrieve by another dog. The blinds may or may not be included in the multiple marked retrieves. There is an additional option of an upland hunting test (not to be confused with the Upland Hunt category), but this is required to be announced in advance of the hunt in the premium (or application) for the test. There is a considerable amount of judges' discretion in the construction of test scenarios at the Finished Hunt. Maximum retrieve test distances at the Finished Hunt level can be considerable. The land maximum distance is one hundred and fifty yards, the water limit is one hundred and twenty-five yards, and the blinds a whopping one hundred yards. These distances are extremely long for a spaniel (or a retriever for that matter). A successful completion of a Finished Hunt level test nets the dog fifteen championship points per Hunt with no specified maximum number of points.

The titles, which appear as prefixes to the dog's UKC-registered name, are awarded on the basis of points. As we have seen, to be awarded the Started Hunting Retriever (SHR) prefix, a dog must have four successful passes of the Started Hunt testing level or 20 points. All of these points must be earned at the Started level.

The next level up, the Hunting Retriever (HR) title can be earned in a number of ways. For example, a dog could first earn a SHR and have 10 points in the bag toward the HR title and then be required to pass the Seasoned Hunt level three times to earn sufficient points for the HR title. But nothing precludes the dog from passing on the SHR title and going directly to the HR title by passing the Seasoned Level four times to amass the necessary points. Finished Hunt successful completions also may be used to complete the HR title requirements. However, here it gets tricky. Once you have earned points through passing a higher level Hunt, you cannot then drop back to the lower level to earn championship points. The requirement for HR is 40 points.

To earn a Hunting Retriever Champion (HRCH) title, a dog must earn 100 points of which 60 points must be earned by passing Finished Hunt tests. The other 40 points can be earned either entirely from Seasoned Hunt tests or from a combination of Started (10 points maximum) and Seasoned (30 points maximum) tests.

To be awarded the Grand Hunting Retriever Champion (GRHRCH) a dog must be virtually capable of walking on water, levitation, and prestidigitation. The dog must have amassed 200 points beyond the HRCH title (a total of 300 points) with 80 of the 200 coming from two successful completions of the Grand Hunt test. These Grand Hunts are held semiannually over a four-day period and are only open to dogs possessing the HRCH title. The remainder of the points must come from successful completions of the Finished Hunt tests. These are highly advanced tests with five events: a multiple marked water retrieve, multiple marked land retrieve, a water blind, a land blind, and an upland game and quartering test. The judging is very tough with callbacks used at each level to reduce the field.

Finally, the UKC sponsors the Upland Hunt designed specifically for the upland game hunting situation. This Hunt consists of walk-up hunt, a quartering test, and optional tracking test. A dog must be steady to flush and shot, demonstrate advanced handling capabilities, and sound retrieving capability. Upon successful completion of four Upland Hunts, a dog may earn the title of Upland Hunter (UH).

Spaniel Breed Organization Working Dog and Working Dog Excellent Certificates: In addition to AKC, NAHRA, and UKC, AKC spaniel parent clubs, such as the English Springer Spaniel Field Trial Association, the English Cocker Spaniel Club of America, the Welsh Springer Spaniel Club of America, and others award Working Dog (WD) and Working Dog Excellent (WDX) certificates following a one-day hunt test. Both certificates are awarded as a result of a common test with the difference between the WD and WDX awards to passing dogs calculated by the judges on the basis of how well a dog passed the test in each category. Essentially the WD and WDX one-day test closely follows the AKC Junior Hunter hunt test for spaniels. The dog must demonstrate basic quartering, handling, and retrieving skills in retrieving two shot birds in the land portion of the test. The standards do not require dogs to be steady to flush and shot. However, a slight difference between the Junior Hunter and WD and WDX land test standards is a dog must be "steady on line" prior to running the water test. This means the dog must sit quietly off lead without breaking prior to the judge giving the handler permission to send the dog on the water retrieve. Birds need not be retrieved to hand, merely to the general vicinity of the handler–usually measured as two large steps–except for the WDX title, which will require a dog to deliver to hand and be line steady at the water.

The second part of the test consists of a water retrieve. Again, the dog must perform a water retrieve very similar to that of the AKC Junior Hunter standards. The standards do not require a dog to be line steady at the water, and like the land portion, the dog is not required to deliver the bird to hand. The difference between WD and WDX is how well the dog performs these tasks. A rough rule of thumb is that a WD award corresponds essentially to what would constitute a successful leg of Junior Hunter test. A WDX award can be likened to how a dog that would successfully pass a leg of the AKC Senior Hunter test would be expected to perform given Junior Hunter standards.

The English Springer Spaniel Field Trial Association in May 2003 adopted a beyond the Master Hunter level test called the Master Hunting Dog Excellent (MHDX) program. It is the only spaniel breed organization at the time of writing to have adopted a program of this level. The MHDX program requires that a dog have an AKC Master Hunter title or at least one point toward its Field Champion or Amateur Field Champion title. The requirements for an MHDX certificate are steep. For the land portion of the test, two dogs are run in a "brace" and must not only be steady to flush and shot, but be capable of honoring the other dog's retrieve (similar to field trial rules). There is a land blind, similar to the AKC Master Hunter standard and a water blind also similar to the AKC Master Hunter standard. Finally, a dog must pass a double marked water retrieve in order to receive the MHDX certificate.

All this hunting and field testing alphabet soup, testing requirements, and points versus legs can make a person's head hurt from seeking to remember all the nuances and terminology. The important thing to remember, however, is that with the AKC, NAHRA, and UKC, there are sufficient tests and titles to keep a spaniel owner occupied for a very long time. At the end of the day these testing standards offer the novice and advanced dog trainer goals and elements of training plan as well as downright fun–the most important part of the hunt test equation.

INTRODUCTION TO FIELD TRIALS AND BASIC FIELD TRIAL HANDLING: Field Trials, the major league events of the gun dog sporting world, are a humbling experience. These are head to head competitions between serious dog owners and handlers and superbly trained gun dogs. The standard gets higher every year with judges demanding, and receiving, incredible performances from dogs and handlers alike. They are also an unbelievably exhilarating experience. Once hooked on the trial circuit with that first ribbon, for many it becomes a life-long addiction.

The two largest flushing dog field trial groups in the United States are the AKC-sponsored English springer spaniel trials amd the English cocker spaniel trials. This is also the case in the United Kingdom. In Canada, however, both springers and cockers may compete against one another in the same trial. Both springer and cocker trials are run in essentially the same manner. Spaniel field trials are generally held in very large areas of knee to waist high brome or switch

FC Priorsmeadow Yasmin MH makes a beautiful delivery to Tony during this field trial. She went on to win the Guns Award at the 2003 National Cocker Championship.

grass fields. Although cocker trials may sometimes vary from the open field approach and have portions of the trial run in the woods.

Trials consist usually of three heats called the first, second, and third series in the field trial lexicon. These series are elimination rounds. Dogs run in a brace of two on a pre-established course. Flags mark the centerline and boundaries of the course, with one dog on each side of the flag centerline constituting the brace. There are two judges, one for each dog, and three gunners–one stationed in the center and two on either side of the central gunner to cover the edges of the field. The gallery, or spectators, are kept under control by the marshal, and follow about ten yards behind the center gunner for safety reasons down the center of the course. Each dog is generally, but not always, required to find, flush, and retrieve two shot birds. To enter a trial a dog must be steady to flush and shot, be capable of honoring another dog's flush and retrieve (which means be steady to flush and shot of other dogs' birds), and retrieve all game that has been shot to hand. Generally, field trials use pheasants or chukar partridge as the game birds of choice, because these birds flush aggressively and pose challenges on retrieves. The bird steward, a highly adventurous soul with perhaps the most hazardous job in the field, must constantly plant birds in advance of the contestants as they move downfield while dodging a rain of lead pellets.

To successfully pass a particular series, a dog must quarter aggressively with panache, not miss any planted birds (called "passed birds"), remain on his course without venturing onto the course of his neighbor to steal or "poach" a bird from his fellow dog, must remain steady to flush and shot on his own course, honor the dog next door under similar circumstances, make retrieves that would cause a Labrador Retriever owner to shiver with delight, be capable of text book blind retrieves, and oh by the way, make it all look very easy and natural. Sounds pretty tough, right? These are merely the entry requirements. Judges will have to make tough choices as to which dog and handler team performs these tasks better than the others.

Each series is an elimination round. Dogs that make it to the next series are called back by the judges to compete in the next round. In the case of springer trials, "call backs" will narrow a field of a sixty-five

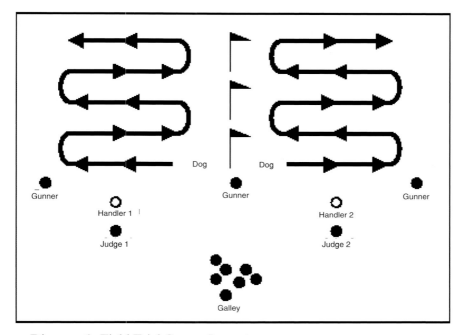

Diagram 6. Field Trial Course Layout.

or so starting dogs to around thirty for the second series. The third series usually consists of around ten to fifteen dogs that vie for four places and a Guns Award. Trials can be serious business, especially in the open category, where professionals compete head to head for the honors and top dogs. At the professional level, it can be intensely competitive with a lot at stake–titles, prestige, and national recognition. The amateurs compete just as fiercely for titles and prestige.

Success in field trials is determined by a variety of variables: the style and determination with which the dog hunts, the ease in which the handler and dog work together, the handler-dog bond, how much the handler needs to make corrective commands, the dog's enthusiasm, the dog's marking and retrieving ability, and those intangible "gut feelings" of the judges. All of these elements combine to make a field trial winner. At the end of the day, it is a unique combination of grit, determination, happenstance, and downright "body english" that often determines a winner when all else is equal. Irrespective of one's assessment of one's dog and handling capabilities, field trials are the quintessential crapshoot. Dogs and people–even great ones–have bad days, and it seems that in field trials the two coincide more than elsewhere. The key is to not let it frustrate you if it happens–and it will happen.

One of the best handling tips for the novice field trialer is to consider the wind. For example, should the wind be at your back, the dog still needs to cover its course. However, at that same time, the dog should be going out at a greater distance in front of you because the only way it can pick up scent is down wind of you. These "down and back" patterns can throw the novice off, because the dog naturally is seeking scent covering as efficiently as possible all the ground between himself and the handler. Wind direction will greatly influence the dog's quartering pattern. You still must keep the dog under control, but the pattern of the dog greatly impacts how it will run that particular series. In the end, however, those who are serious gun dog owners, trainers, and handlers, will gravitate toward the field trial circuit–its rewards and its heartbreaks are the stuff of the gun dog world. Success in field trials is predicated upon having an extremely well-trained dog and talented dog, and being an experienced handler. The first two elements are self-evident. Entering a field trial with an untrained dog is a waste of time, money, and effort. Similarly, even the most inexperienced trainer can tell if his or her dog has the "right stuff." Handling or "driving" as we like to call it, is much more difficult for the novice to evaluate because, as in all things, it is extremely hard for an individual to evaluate his or her capabilities while handling a dog.

Handling is more than just walking behind your dog tooting your whistle. It is a job that requires you to be two steps ahead of your dog at all times. You need to know how your dog will react to certain situations as they arise during a trial. It is virtually certain "Murphy's Law" will be the governing force behind one's participation in field trials. What can go wrong will almost always happen. For example, a bird is shot from the other course eight feet from your dog's head, what do you do? Do you allow the dog to break and retrieve it? Or you encounter a pheasant running toward the centerline of the trial course. Do you stop the dog or hope it produces the bird before he reaches the centerline, or do you call the dog off the bird? The proper course of action is rarely self-evident and in fact may vary according to the field, the judges, and the dog's performance that day. A tip here is to communicate with the judge as you proceed down the course and let the judge make the decision as to allow you to go over the line or not. Most judges will evaluate the situation and tell you how they wish your dog to handle a field problem.

Field trials are an exhilarating experience, the highs are very high; the lows, however, are very low. Our best advice is to rely upon your professional trainer to show you the field trial ropes. Learning as you go, or through the school of "hard knocks," takes far longer to turn you into a sound field trial handler. One approach is to let your professional handle your dog through a couple of trials as you study the professional's technique. Once you are comfortable with the trial setting and have an appreciation of the intricacies of the inner-workings of a field trial, try your hand at driving your dog.

The next half of this chapter will focus on handling for the field and hunt test using vignettes–some true and some fictitious–to provide novice and experienced handler alike with some solid tips on handling for hunt test situations, field trials, and the field.

NOVICE HUNT TEST HANDLING: It was cold but sunny, with a biting wind that blew through the mountains of Western Pennsylvania this second day of a two-day hunt test. A determined novice handler had successfully negotiated the perils of the land portion of the Junior Hunt test in the morning and was poised at the water with his young springer "hupped" at his side, the British-style slip lead loosely encircling the neck of this talented, but raw female spaniel. He was apprehensive. The previous day the dog had not made the cut to proceed to the water portion of the test–failing the land test because she had hunted "out of control" in a wind that blew from almost directly behind the handler. She, in fact, had quartered superbly taking full advantage of the wind, despite the driving sleet to find, flush, and retrieve two shot chukar partridges. It was the inexperience of the handler, not the dog's performance, that had resulted in a failing score that day. Rather than moving briskly forward to keep the guns in range, our hero had moved tentatively, as if his feet were encased in concrete.

The guns, true to form, remained even with the handler. The dog patterned beautifully, in a downwind pattern in long loping strides that took full advantage of the wind. She did this instinctively, not as a result of any direction from the handler. As a result, the springer flushed the birds well, but essentially out of good shooting range. The guns made the equivalent of a "diving catch in the end zone." The judges made the correct call. "Just a little raw…" one judge told the handler "….all that is needed is a little more practice." Months later after sober reflection, the handler was not certain if the judge was talking about him or the dog.

Today, however, this was all history. The chief judge instructed the handler, "your dog does not have to be steady to wing and shot. You may restrain her loosely with the lead. She does not have to retrieve to hand, but must bring the bird to within two steps of you." The bird throwers were positioned some forty plus yards away on a bank of this oval-shaped pond about half way to the far end of the pond. With them was an Adirondack basket filled to the brim with recently shot chukars; they awaited the signal from the judge. With a nod of the judge's head, one man threw the bird approximately thirty yards in front of the dog as his companion fired a shotgun to simulate the downing of a bird in flight. The judge tapped the handler on the shoulder and he gave the retrieve command. "Dixie," the handler said quietly.

The springer, an aggressive retriever and an excellent marker, exploded off the bank and hit the icy cold waters of the pond. The intense cold of the water took the young dog's breath away and she began to flail her front paws instantly in reaction to the frigid water temperature; her flailing kicking up sufficient water in front of her that she was not able to keep a firm visual or scent fix on the location of the floating bird. She began to veer away from the bird and return to the handler. Our novice handler, heart in his throat, sought to recall the dog, but she ignored him, returning to shore and climbing out of the water. She looked briefly at the handler, sniffed indifferently at several decoys, and then trotted around the bank of the pond toward the bird throwers and the big basket of birds. Our handler, in a unique moment of clarity, elected not to recall the dog once more and ceased his efforts to control her, fearing that all was lost.

The young springer greeted the bird throwers enthusiastically, sniffed at the bird basket with a distinct lack of interest, turned toward the water and spotted her bird floating twenty yards away in middle of the pond. To the amazement of the handler, judges, gallery, and the bird throwers, the springer launched herself at the floating bird, this time quickly covering the distance separating her from her prize, seized the bird in her mouth, turned left, and briskly swam the thirty yards separating her from the handler. She scrambled out of the water onto bank a yard or so away from the handler, put the bird down and shook herself vigorously. The handler was beside himself with tension, but he gave her no commands. In what seemed to the handler an eternity, the springer calmly picked the bird back up and delivered it to the handler's hand. The judge looked the novice in the eye as he handed her the bird, saying evenly, "… a most unusual retrieve." The handler thanked the judge, but made no further comment. As he slipped the English-style slip lead over the springer's head and made his way to his place in the gallery, a seasoned veteran of the field trial and hunt test circuit waiting to run a young dog said, "Chip, that dog really saved your ass." Not usually known for quick comebacks, the handler quipped, "There is nothing like training," but in his heart he knew that she had him dead to rights. He was still musing on that exchange when the judges called out the qualifying dogs for that day and handed him his ribbon.

Several handling lessons emerge from this true story that can assist the novice handler.

✦ Carefully consider wind direction and its impact on your spaniel's hunting style during all phases of a hunt or field test. Adjust your pace during the land series to keep pace with your dog's progress downfield so as to keep your dog within shooting range; the guns only move with the handler.

✦ Do not "over handle" your dog; when it appears that things are going to "hell in a hand basket." Sometimes allowing the dog to do what a dog does naturally will actually save the day.

✦ Do not discuss your dog's performance with a judge at any time during the hunt test; you may be doing better than you think. Never argue with a judge.

✦ Always, always thank the judge and your guns after you run a leg.

INTERMEDIATE HUNT TEST HANDING: It was a typical cold, soggy, and overcast Mid-Atlantic region early spring day–the first day of a two-day hunt test. The morning dew had soaked through the handler's pants and contributed a chill that his morning coffee had done little to diminish. The marshal had called for him, dog number 4 in the Senior Hunter lineup. This was the start of the field portion of the test. He was a curious mixture of confidence and mild detachment topped off with minor anxiety, and was ready to get the field test part out of the way. Already looking forward, with not a little trepidation, toward the Senior Hunter "hunt dead," he jumped slightly as one of the judges tapped him on the shoulder and explained the rules on the field test. "Your cocker must demonstrate good bird-finding skills beyond the junior level. She does not have to be steady to wing and shot, but must retrieve to hand. We are looking for solid control, good coverage of the field, and responsiveness. You must not use excessive commands to call her off a fly-away bird." The handler nodded. He thought his girl could do all that well, given that he had sent her off for a month to his professional trainer. He had not had a chance to work much with the little cocker; he had only picked her up from the trainer a few days previously, but he was not concerned. He had watched the trainer run her through her paces on several shot birds, a couple of hunt deads, and some water retrieves. She had performed flawlessly and was, in fact, steady to wing and shot–a true rock.

With a nod from the judge, he "hupped" her, and then sent her out. She began working the field very well, taking full advantage of the good scenting conditions as she worked into a slightly gusting, quartering wind from the left. She made a solid find of her first chukar, flushed it and hupped at the flush..."near perfect", the handler thought. The bird flushed, caught a gust, and the gun on the right side missed with both barrels what can only be described as a near perfect set up–the gunner would think hard on that one this evening. The little cocker broke from her hup, obviously chagrined at the gunner's lack of skill. The handler tooted vigorously on his whistle, but she ignored him plowing ever further through the knee-high weeds in search of the flyaway bird. The handler yelled "here" and "gone away" until he was blue in the face. After a while, the judge tapped him on the shoulder and suggested kindly he collect his dog. The dejected handler hoped for a better showing the next day.

Dawn the following day broke cold and clear, but a hard frost on the ground remained throughout the morning. The handler was pleased with his dog's performance. The young cocker had performed much better in the land series and had managed a credible retrieve during the Senior Hunter "hunt dead." She was now at the on line at the water, " hupped" directly in front of our handler. The handler, as ready as he ever would be he thought, nodded that he was set to the judge. The judge signaled the bird stewards and one steward threw the dead bird as the second steward fired the shotgun to simulate a shot bird. The young spaniel's eyes blazed intensely as she spotted the bird in flight. The handler, positioned behind the dog, could not see the telltale signs that she was about to lose control. The cocker exploded off the line charging aggressively into the water in pursuit of the downed bird. The judge had yet to tap the handler on the shoulder–a sign that he could release the dog for the retrieve. Our handler again was disappointed.

Our fictional handler had just made several mistakes that any relatively inexperienced handler might make at the Senior Hunter level. One of these is extremely common as gun dog owners seek to move from one hunt test level to the next. Many handlers routinely send their dogs out to professional trainers in advance of the hunt test season to be "steadied" and gain experience in field work sufficient to pass the Senior Hunt Test. Just as many fail to follow up that training by working with the dog prior to the test.

+ Spend as much time handling your dog in various scenarios after you pick him up from the trainer, but before both you are in a hunt test situation. Many urban dog owners assume their dogs will handle for them the way they did for the professional trainer. Sometimes they do....most of the

155

time they do not. The whistle peeps, body language, and handling style of the owner will be quite different from that of the professional.

✦ Make sure when a dog must be line steady, as in the AKC Senior or Master Hunter water retrieve or the NAHRA Intermediate Test, that you position yourself immediately to the side of your dog, so as to be in a position to "control him." Without touching him, talking to him, or using hand gestures to restrain him, your body position exerts a powerful restraining influence on a dog if he can see you.

✦ Practicing line-steadying drills under a variety of conditions is essential to ensure your spaniel does not break at the intermediate level.

Advanced Handling: The judge, highly experienced in hunt tests, and AKC, UKC, and NAHRA certified to judge the full range of hunt tests, walked up to the handler. With a wind-weathered and heavily callused hand from years of working spaniels and retrievers on checkcords, the mid-westerner pointed the course out to the handler and gave him final instructions on this part of the land portion of the Master Hunt Test for spaniels. It was a glorious upper mid-western day for the test.

The course layout for the day's test was on difficult terrain–a rolling hill that formed a plateau about fifty yards down the field, which sloped sharply downhill to the left. A pond formed the leftmost boundary of the course. There was a left cheek wind (the wind was a crosswind going from left to right). The handler, studying the dog for a moment to ensure that he and the dog were connected, cast the dog off to the left into the wind. The cast caused the dog to drift too far to the left field, visibly failing to cover adequately the far right and middle portions of the course. The handler, failing to correct his initial mistake, made a futile effort to handle the dog back to the right so the dog could adequately cover the course. Focused on the dog's performance, the handler stumbled across a chukar planted in the central part of the course and flushed the bird. The judge tapped the handler on the shoulder and requested him to pick up his dog. At the Master

Hunter level, a passed bird is a serious error that if repeated would doom a dog's chances.

+ Carefully study the course, terrain, and wind to determine the best path for your dog down the course. Compensate for wind and terrain in your initial cast of the dog. In the example above, dogs naturally drift downhill and into the wind. A right cast might have saved the day.

+ Do your best to recover from a bad cast. If necessary recall the dog and start the run over. You might lose some points, but you might pass that portion of the test.

+ Wind and terrain come into play heavily during the Master Hunter hunt dead and the water blind retrieve. Make certain you compensate for the wind and consider terrain when lining your dog up for the retrieve in both of these tests. In other words if the wind is coming across your right cheek and the judge is telling you the bird is basically straight out in front of you by a tree, you have to think about your dog and that he will not scent it if he goes left of the tree; he needs to go a bit right of the tree to scent the bird, so line your dog up a bit right of that tree. Then the dog will go more or less straight out, but when he hits that scent cone, your puppy will spin his head around on the scent and make the retrieve. This makes you look very good, like an experienced, smart handler.

The Joy of Hunting with Your Spaniel or Retriever: The ultimate goal of all of this training, hunt testing, and field trialing really is to get your dog in top notch hunting condition for those fall days all of us await with anxious anticipation. A trip to South Dakota to shoot ringneck pheasants, to northern Minnesota, Wisconsin, or Michigan for grouse, or to Montana for sharptails, prairie chickens, Hungarian partridge, and pheasants is the objective of virtually all that train sporting dogs. With that in mind, we have sought to outline several things to consider while hunting your favorite bird that will enable your flushing dog to perform to the best of his ability:

Roettger Ridge's Rivendell on the hunt. (Photo by Tony Roettger).

Pheasant, Prairie Chickens, and Sharptail Grouse Hunting: Hunting pheasants, prairie chickens, or sharptail grouse with a superbly trained spaniel or retriever from our perspective is the penultimate hunting experience a person can have with his or her dog. To make this hunt the memorable experience that you and your comrades wish it to be, there a several things to consider while hunting with your four-legged friend. A flushing dog hunts best in prairie grass, fallow farmland (Conservation Reserve Program or CRP land as it is called), or in the woods (especially for English cockers). In the vastness of the mid-western plains, especially in what constitutes the corn-belt of the United States, pheasant hunters often seek to run spaniels or retrievers in cornfields as part of the classic team shooting of walkers and blockers stationed at the end of the field. Flushing dogs unused to cornfields have a difficult time with them. They start out quartering well for about one to two turns, but when they spot a pheasant, they will take off running after it. Pheasants, on the other hand, dearly love cornfields. They view the endless cornrows as something akin to

A beautiful Chesapeake Bay retriever, GMHR, WR, SR Tugboats Ironwood Lap CD, JH, MH, CGC, TDI "Ferrous" owned by Bradley L. Sisson, makes a fine retrieve of this duck. (Photo by Hannu Eloranta).

a drag strip. A pheasant in a cornrow will take off running right down the row (that is why the blockers are stationed at the end) with the dog in hot pursuit. If this occurs early on in the cornfield, which can stretch for almost a mile, the dog will flush every bird while he pursues that single pheasant well out of range of your gun. The result is a less than rewarding hunt. Try to stay clear of the cornfields while hunting with your spaniel or your retriever unless you have trained him specifically to hunt them.

Fences, as we discussed previously in Chapter 7, also offer a distinct challenge to flushing dogs not used to hunting along a fence line. The same runner phenomenon will occur as the pheasant, desperate to escape the determined dog, runs along the fence line. The result, especially if the dog is unsteady, is a madcap chase, where the dog soon vanishes from sight. Stick to the CRP land if your dog has never hunted the cornfields or the fence lines, or if you are uncertain as to your ability to control him.

The wind is a distinct challenge in the openness of the mid-western plains. It sometimes blows with a ferocity that befuddles the mind. Assess wind direction and try if possible to hunt with your four-legged friend in a crosswind. Hunting initially in a crosswind will be easier for you both, as it will cause your dog to hunt more closely to you. A down wind pattern will make your friend hunt farther away from you, because he will need to be in front of you to find the birds between you and him. If you have to hunt downwind with your dog, try to keep him in somewhat close, but more importantly, under control. If he is hunting too wide, a bit deep, and slightly out of range, you have a couple of options to bring him under control. The first approach is merely to follow him until the dog eventually wears out. Once tired, dogs generally listen to commands and tend to obey better than when they are "fresh out of the box." Try this approach if you are only able to hunt with your dog only three or four times a year, and by golly want to shoot some birds.

If you hunt more frequently, the second approach is to lift the dog off the ground and shake him up. When lifted off the ground, dogs often tend to become a little disoriented and hence a little more submissive. Try hunting him again. If this does not work, you may be better off putting him back in the car for a bit. Take him out later in the day. If he still does not come around, put him up for the day. If he is hunting out of control, a pheasant flushed in a high wind downwind of you likely will result in your highly trained field-bred champion giving the bird the chase of its life completely oblivious to your frantic whistles and sharp voice commands. Dogs, after all, have bad days just as we humans do.

Grouse hunting: Flushing dogs are superb on grouse. Grouse, however, cherish a habitat that poses distinct difficulties for man and dog. Blackberry bushes with their murderous thorns, thick young aspen fields with their closely packed trees and scrub bushes, and heavily forested areas with thick undergrowth and poor shooting lanes, are all places that grouse call home. Handling your spaniel or retriever in dense cover while waiting for that sudden explosion so typical of a ruffed grouse flush demands much. Grouse hunting with a flushing dog is very challenging, but it is the height of fun. In thick cover, where grouse tend to live, your dog needs to hunt very close to you. Even with a close working dog, you will likely hear and possibly see a few grouse. With dense cover, however, you may or may not have an unobstructed shot. The best trick we have found for hunting grouse in heavy cover is to watch the dog. When the dog gets an obvious bird scent, you need to try to position yourself toward what you may think of as the direction the birds will fly. Grouse hunting with flushing dogs requires quick reflexes and an ability to move quickly once the dog gets "birdy." Tarry not, or the dog will flush the grouse before you are in position. Grouse are notorious for flying behind trees just as you are about to shoot, so stay close to the dog and hope for a good shot. The authors, hunting spaniels in a brace last year in thick cover on a beautiful fall day in Northern Minnesota came up empty handed after multiple grouse flushes. We moved just that bit too slow.

Waterfowl: A spaniel or a retriever is as near to the all-purpose dog as one can get. Wonderful dogs on upland game birds, they also excel as retrievers on waterfowl when hunting from a blind. To be a successful dog in a hunting blind, you must have trained your dog as a non-slip retriever. To situate a young spaniel or retriever, not "place" trained in a hunting blind with two of your best friends, coffee, donuts, shells, guns, and all of the accoutrements, is to court disaster. It probably will be the last time you receive an invitation to join them in pursuit of geese and ducks. Spaniels and retrievers (spaniels a little more than retrievers) have an intense genetic pre-disposition to quarter and move to flush game. To temper this, you need to concentrate on developing control with your dog so that he will be able to spend those hours in the blind without driving you and your friends mad. We discussed those advanced retriever training techniques in detail in Chapter 6. Your dog must be capable of double and triple marks and taking a solid line when sent for a retrieve. Remember, spaniels lack the natural coat and skin oil retrievers have to protect them from bitterly cold waters. If you choose to hunt with a spaniel in extreme conditions, use a neoprene vest with floatation to ensure that your dog does not succumb to hypothermia or leave him at home.

+ When you are finished with your hunt, make sure that your dog gets a dry, sheltered place to rest with plenty of food and water. Some tricks to get your dog trained to stay put in the blind are to keep a lead on your dog0 until he begins to realize that if he stays in the blind, the ducks will come to him, and he does not need to hunt them up as he was taught to do for upland birds.

+ If you are hunting with friends, a good tip is for you not to shoot the first few birds. Instead concentrate on controlling your dog and let your buddies shoot the first couple until your puppy begins to watch the sky for those incoming mallards or teal. Once your four-legged friend understands he must wait in the blind quietly watching for the ducks to fly to him before he gets the retrieve, he will be a sound waterfowling partner for those early season duck hunts from a blind.

Jump-shooting ducks and geese along streams and ponds with your spaniel or retriever is a time-honored American tradition. Again, control and training are the keys to a successful hunt. Your dog's heeling ability is a critical element to your success in jump-shooting ducks. To sneak up on the ducks and not have the dog scare the heck out of them while you are still crouched down in the weeds or hiding behind the trees, your dog must be under control and at heel until sent for a retrieve. This may be difficult for that hard-charging spaniel that resists heeling; however, you need to work as a team for this to be successful. The best approach is to heel your dog as you are crouched down and slowly sneak up on these ducks staying as low to the ground as possible. When you get into a good shooting position, unleash your puppy if you had him on a lead or just "hup" him if he is steady and wait until you have finished shooting – there is generally no flushing done in jump shooting ducks. He should be in an excellent position to retrieve the downed birds. Hopefully you have done some blind retrieve work as well, in case he is not able to get a clear mark on the ducks you have shot, so you are able to put those in the game bag.

Doves: Down South, where homemade biscuits, Virginia ham, and grits are the norm for a hunter's breakfast, the doves fly fast and hot in the early September mornings and late afternoons. For states that consider doves a game bird (mostly in the South and lower mid-west) the early September dove season is a much anticipated and coveted time of the year. Spaniels and retrievers are well suited to flushing doves in fields and, as with waterfowl hunting from blinds, can function nicely as non-slip retrievers for dove shoots. The same training and handling regimes apply for dove hunting as for waterfowl hunting. However, because of the extremely high temperatures encountered in early September, hunters must take extra precautions to ensure their dogs do not fall prey to heat injuries, which in extreme instances can lead to the death of the dog. Take plenty of water for you and your dog. Cool the dog off in ponds with a couple of mid-day tosses of the dummy. Limit your hunting times accordingly, and when in doubt, leave the dog at home.

If hunting is your primary goal, you may use any of the techniques in this book to get your dog in shape for that fall hunting. Even if all you do is hunt, tuning up your dog and keeping him in shape in the off-season should be a primary goal. It is so important you throw some dummies, practice a few drills, and take a turn or two through the fields to maintain his level of proficiency. Take him swimming; work on some advanced retrieving skills. A little off-season work will make that hunting trip all the more enjoyable.

A very successful day in the field. Lola is owned by Wes Riffel.
(Photo by Wes Riffel).

NINE

Flushing Dogs and their Problems

An **Ounce of Prevention:** The best way to cure problems associated with flushing dogs is to nip them in the bud before they happen. If you followed the approach we have outlined throughout this book, you will find that selecting the right dog at the outset combined with consistency, patience, reading your dog, not pressing a dog to move to another level before he is ready, praise, reward, and a lot of pure unadulterated love goes a long way toward preventing problems in spaniels or retrievers. We also recognize that, despite our very best efforts, certain gun dogs with impeccable breeding, superb training, nurturing, and a lot of love will develop some problems. This chapter is not designed to be the ultimate word in dealing with the very broad topic of solving flushing dog problems. It is our intent to explore some of the basic and more correctable problems that are often encountered with flushing dogs and offer some observations on how they can be mitigated.

Basic flushing dog troubles fall into several categories: hardmouth, retrieving and delivery problems, and control problems that we will address in this chapter. Correction of fundamental canine behavioral problems, such as excessive chewing, pacing, and uncontrolled barking, is rightfully the preserve of veterinarians and animal behaviorists and is beyond the scope of this work. Concomitantly, veterinarians and animal behaviorialists tend to be somewhat out of their elements with hunting problems, unless of course they hunt and train with flushing dogs. When spaniels or retrievers exhibit problems that defy the amateur trainer's capabilities to correct, the best recourse is the professional. However, there are certain techniques the determined amateur can utilize to reduce or eliminate basic problems.

Hardmouth: Hardmouth is to a great extent subjective. It has received notoriety of late as a result of hunt test or field trial judging standards. For example, the AKC rules for hunt tests is "fit for table," and we actually like this as it forces the judge to decide as to the edibility of the bird. In essence, this ruling gives wide latitude to the judges as to what does and does not constitute hardmouth for hunt test purposes. There are at least two root causes of hardmouth that we can identify–learned behavior and genetics. In the case of field-bred spaniels and retrievers, we believe that the former is far more common than the latter.

Learned hardmouth can have its origins early in a puppy's life. Squeaky toys for puppies are one of the worst creators of hardmouth, we believe. In essence, a squeaky toy rewards the puppy for biting down on the toy through–you guessed it–the squeak the toy gives off. As the dog grows older and begins to work on birds, he will find that certain birds, such as quail, chukar partridge, and pheasants, give off a squeak if squeezed by the dog's jaws.

We have also found that playing tug of war with a young puppy is also potential cause of hardmouth. Here the reward is in the competition over an item and fun and attention the puppy receives from you in return. Later on in his career, he will seek to play tug of war with shot game, instead of delivering that nice mallard duck you just shot.

Sometimes you run across cases of hardmouth that have occurred in older dogs. An older dog used to heavy fieldwork that grows tired of being whacked in the head by pheasant wings or spurred in the mouth by a cock bird sometimes will solve the problem by developing a case of hardmouth. We have seen dogs that have learned how to dispatch a bird quite efficiently. There was a particular case of an older dog that would give a bird a quick fang through the head if she could catch or trap a bird on the ground–efficient, intelligent, and learned. In these instances behavior–not breeding–is the issue. Although we did not go into force breaking in this book, professionals have had some success in "force breaking in reverse" to attempt to correct this problem. In other words administer the pressure on the ear when the dog bites down hard. Some dogs do the damage to the bird during the pick up of the bird but not while carrying it so you can overcome some instances of hardmouth by convincing the dog to pick up the bird quicker. It is our opinion that any attempt to correct hardmouth really only masks the issue. It's highly likely the dog will never be completely cured of the problem.

Without a doubt, there are some dogs that naturally have a hard mouth. This is why breeding is such a critical element in the equation. Dogs that are born with hardmouth will generally always kill birds, and there is little one can do about it, short of giving the dog away and starting over. Some dogs will kill birds in such a fashion as to leave no mark on the bird; others may chew birds to pieces or even eat them. Dogs that merely kill birds are not necessarily bad dogs; if your objective is a good field dog for those Saturday afternoon hunts, then this should not matter at all. Many good field trial wash outs just simply give a bit of a tight squeeze that cause the death of a bird, so they cannot compete. In most cases they make fantastic hunt test and gun dogs. However, dogs that chew up game or eat it are not useful as gun dogs. Should you have one of these, they are better left out of the field.

Adolescent Retrieving Games and Delivery Problems: At an early age, a young dog may still exhibit some puppy-specific problems in delivery such as playing with the dummy, not bringing it directly to you, unwillingness to relinquish the bird (as opposed to hardmouth), or perhaps a little "come chase me and get the bird" games. These are all little quirks that generally disappear with the passage of time as the dog matures. We have found using a tough approach with puppies that tend to be a little more playful in their retrieves probably creates more problems than it solves in the long run.

Sometimes, however, there are basic delivery issues that need to be addressed before the dog can perform suitably in the field, hunt tests, or field trials. If a dog still exhibits some of these traits after it is about eighteen months old, you may wish to try the following. If a dog is marking and retrieving well, but is shying away from you in its delivery or dropping the bird or dummy before it gets to you, drop to one knee lower your eyes when he makes the approach to you. Encourage the dog to come to you and when it gets to you do not take the dummy or bird from it. Instead, give the "hup" command or just hold onto dog telling him he is such a good boy (sometimes "hup" will make him drop it...not always just sometimes), stroke the dog, and shower it with praises. Allow him to keep the dummy for a period of time. You may even wish to put the lead on the dog and "heel" him for a while all the time allowing the dog to have the dummy. After few minutes, give the "drop" command and take the dummy. Immediately give the dummy back to the dog.

Repeat this process several times praising the dog. Patience, practice, encouragement, and a little time generally is all that is needed to correct these issues and have a dog that delivers a bird or dummy to hand every time. Remember, the dog's reward is the retrieve of the bird. Allow him to be proud of the bird and enjoy it; do not be in a hurry to take it away. This will ensure a clean, snappy delivery in a good natural retriever for the life of the dog. An additional approach is to use the checkcord to correct the problem of the dog not returning directly to you or taking a looping pattern to deliver the bird to your hand. The key to doing this, though, is do not nag the dog with the checkcord. Remember to pop that cord slightly and say "here" at the same time to obtain the desired result. A problem with the checkcord approach is sometimes dogs will drop the bird if you snap the cord too hard. Use your best judgment when it comes to how hard you pop that cord. Ideally, you want the dog to look at you, and then you say "here" again. In most cases, the pup will come to you. Other methods used for a dog that resists returning directly to you would be: if the dog keeps a real good hold of the bird or dummy, leave a check cord on for insurance reasons to catch him if need be. Actually go get the dog and with dummy in mouth scruff him and bring him to you a few feet saying "here." Let him sit a minute, and then give him the voice and whistle "here" commands. A few times of this and your dog should get the idea that he needs to come to you directly–not by way of Katmandu. A key to re-enforce this is to give him another retrieve immediately, so he learns that the sooner he gets the bird or dummy back to you, the sooner he can get another retrieve.

Not Retrieving: If your dog flat out refuses to retrieve any object, as is sometimes the case with dogs from poor breeding, you are faced with the prospect of having your dog undergo training designed to instill this drive or abandon any hopes you might have for the dog in the field. A primary use of spaniels and retrievers as gun dogs is their innately strong retrieving drive hunters use to conserve game. There are many different names for the process of training a dog to pick up an object and return to you with it securely in his mouth–conditioned retrieve, force fetching, the forced retrieve, or the trained retrieve. To complicate matters even more, there are perhaps more training techniques and combinations of techniques than names of the process–ear pinch, toe hitch, the eCollar, and the "soft" technique. To make matters worse, the gun dog training world is somewhat divided on the necessity to use the trained retrieve on spaniels and retrievers (although it appears more retriever trainers use the technique than spaniel trainers). Some trainers routinely place all of their dogs on the force-fetching bench. Other trainers may never use the technique to train their charges under the assumption if you have use the technique, the dog is probably not worth much in the field to begin with. Most trainers fall somewhere between these two extremes, and reserve the technique (whichever one they subscribe to) only for those very difficult dogs. It is an area we do not plan to address in this edition. There are several good books on the topic, but our basic advice for fixing retrieving issues associated with either breed is to contact a professional trainer skilled in a range of trained retrieve methods and discuss the problem with the pro. It is possible the retrieving issue can be solved without resorting to a full-blown trained retrieve program. In general, we adhere to the "soft technique" or modified ear pinch when conducting the trained retrieve. The best bet here for the novice, however, is the professional. We discussed in our chapter on selecting the right professional to help you deal with or correct problem areas in your gun dog's training. In selecting the right professional to help with a trained retrieve problem, we believe that it is essential that you match up spaniels with spaniel professionals and retrievers with retriever professionals. Retriever and spaniel professionals employ different trained retrieve techniques consistent with the requirements of their respective breeds.

Marking: Usually, however, poor marking, especially of dummies and birds beyond fifty yards is a result of little practice at these ranges. Trainers often ascribe poor marking skills to dogs that begin to hunt after thirty or forty yards on what is a much longer retrieve. In reality we believe poor marking on the part of the dog has much more to do with the natural limits of the human throwing arm. Try to practice on longer-range retrieves. Station someone seventy to one hundred yards out with a dummy and instruct the person to throw the dummy when you raise your hand. Closely observe the dog's eyes when you give the signal to toss the dummy. Did he register the dummy in the air? If he did, it is probably not a marking problem and can be corrected with a heavy dose of practice on longer retrieves, but not to the point of boredom. You must be sure your dog is having a good time, or he will eventually mismark the fall of the bird or dummy just to entertain himself. Keep the sessions very short, if he is not enthusiastic about the retrieving job. If you have a good dog from good stock, you will already have a good natural retriever that will want to retrieve all day long, so boredom should not be much of an issue

Try as they might, however, some dogs for whatever reason–poor eyesight, wretched attention span, bad memory or pure boredom–are not good markers. For better or worse, genetics are everything, and like it or not, we cannot get around that fact. If you have poor genetics, you are going to get a mediocre to poor dog. The problem is how we define "good." Very simply, a dog is good if you think it is good. If the dog does what you expect it to do when you expect it, then by definition it is good. Professional dog trainers see many good dogs, some great ones. However, many dogs that may be mediocre in the eye of the professional may in fact be the greatest thing to the average hunter. The dog that does its job is a good dog.

Taking Signals on Blind Retrieves and Hunt Deads: If a dog re-fuses to take hand signals on a blind retrieve or hunt dead, chances are fairly good this is a trust issue and he likely is ignoring your commands with the conviction that his nose is better than your brains. Our recommendation for this is to practice the drills in Chapter 6 dealing with advanced retriever drills for blind retrieves and hunt deads. Only when the dog fully equates following your hand signal to finding and retrieving a bird or dummy every time will he begin to trust your hand signal over his instinct. In some dogs, this is quickly learned; in other dogs, it takes months of practice. Make sure the dog is *not* moving when you give an "over" or a "back" command–a moving dog cannot sort out what you want the dog to do. A "hupped" dog can sort your directions. Frequently there are more handler problems than dog problems in this area.

Quartering: The biggest problem we encounter here is when a dog ranges too far for the gunner to make an effective shot. Often we see this trait in big, hard running, and confident dogs–such as some English springers and English cockers. This is a learned attribute; dogs that exhibit this trait are generally strong-willed and very self-assured. They tend also to disregard completely your whistle commands to turn, "hup," or come to you. The result is they find birds at a distance that is not possible for the average hunter to shoot flying birds with the slightest chance of success. If you are blessed (or cursed) with a highly confident hard-charger, spend more time just quartering in the field, merely getting the dog comfortable with whistle commands. If you find he completely disregards your commands and continues to quarter out of range despite your efforts, you might try a checkcord. However, it is likely a checkcord may be a short-lived cure. Highly confident hard running dogs tend to be very intelligent. They know when they are wearing the checkcord and when they are not; the result is they behave accordingly. Your best bet is to continue practice quartering and turning drills. Ultimately, your dog will come around. You might also try carrying a pigeon or dummy in your vest and throwing it a short distance from you when the dog is hunting too far out. This often pulls the dog in closer. Plan the placement of your first dummy or pigeon so that you plant it very close to you. Your dog needs to be convinced birds are always close to you –not seventy yards down the field or in the county. If you always put your dummies far downfield, your dog will begin to think this is where he will always find birds. The reward is the bird, so if he finds birds at a great distance, then he is doing it right in his mind.

Breaking at the fall: Breaking at the fall is a very common problem once a dog knows he wants that bird for a retrieve. If you think about this undesirable trait from the dog's perspective, it has inherent logic. All your puppy wants to do is get that bird for you. We clearly do not want him *not* to stop retrieving, so the cure for fixing this problem can be tricky. You have to think of how soft- or hardheaded the dog is, and that is often very difficult for an amateur or first-time dog owner to ascertain. A good way to assess this is to think about how you started steadying the dog to flush and shot. Did you merely say "Ahhhh" and the puppy stopped? Or did you have to actually physically catch the dog and bring him back to the spot from whence he broke? To fix the problem of the dog breaking at the fall of the bird or dummy, go back to how you taught him not to break when the dummy was thrown. Practice this until the dog clearly has regained his steadiness to thrown dummies and gradually incorporate longer throws that simulate a fallen bird.

Breaking at the Shot: This is almost identical to breaking at the fall of the bird, and needs to be remedied in the same manner. Remember the dog needs to listen to you and retrieve the bird only on your command. He should not be allowed to "assume" that you would send him. That is why you must teach the dog the gunshot is yet another "hup" command very similar to the whistle command. We knew a handler from the deep South who would enter his in cocker in hunt tests and some Trials. She was rock steady to flush and shot, but she would just leave that tiniest bit early when the whistle fell from the handler's mouth so he could call her name for the retrieve. How does one solve that problem? In the same fashion we solved the previous issues. This dog counted or timed her leaving to make the retrieve on that clank of the dropped whistles; she was trained or trained herself to do this.

Excessive Chasing of Birds and Failure to Stop on Command: If you have carefully followed this training guide, this should not be a problem. However, there are some dogs that, when faced with the heady aroma of bird scent, just defy your best abilities to control them. In this instance, the primary recourse is to ensure your dog is steady to flush and shot. This can be a tough problem to correct without help. Our best advice is seek professional help sooner rather than later to correct this problem.

Fear of Water: We covered the introduction to the water extensively in Chapter 5. However, sometimes a puppy's first meeting with the water does not go according to plan. We have received dogs that have had a harsh introduction to water, sometimes a first swim totally unintended by the owner. For example, in one case while the owner was at work, one of his children, no doubt momentarily possessed of some demonic desire to "see what the puppy could do in the water" tossed a young dog unceremoniously into a frigid lake. Naturally the puppy sputtered and fought to get out of the icy cold water. Later that evening, our young devil, shorn of forked tail, horns, and pitchfork and now attired with angelic wings, confessed to his father the dastardly deed. However, the damage was done. The puppy has a lasting fear of water that may or may not be overcome through months of hard work—the verdict is still out.

Another example was a dog that came to us after a trainer, seeking to train the dog to swim by way of canoeing the young puppy to an island in the middle of the pond and marooning the dog there; her only hope of escape from Devil's Island was to swim the distance of the pond back to shore. After this experience, she would not swim to save her life. It took four months of training on birds first to instill in her a desire to retrieve birds, and then this love of bird retrieving was used to overcome her fear of the water. She is now totally at home swimming. Both of these stories underscore it is far harder to overcome a fear of the water than to prevent one from forming. In this instance, an ounce of prevention is definitely worth a pound of cure. However, a hard retrieving drive is about the best thing we have found to overcome a dog's reluctance to swim. We suggest that you work on that first then return to the water. If the dog becomes scared of the water but loves birds, clip wing a pigeon and let it flap across the top of the water. The puppy will hardly be able to resist this temptation in most cases.

A Word about the eCollar: The modern electronic collar, not the older version designed to turn a Golden Retriever's hair as frizzy as a Standard Poodle's is a great tool when used correctly by knowledge-able professional and amateur trainers schooled in its use to correct extremely difficult issues. However, we believe it should not be used as *a primary method* to "train" flushing dogs. This stems in part from our belief that in the hands of the unskilled amateur, it likely will create more problems than it will solve. We also are a bit old fashioned about training and feel many good spaniels and retrievers were trained prior to the advent of the eCollar. Although we believe the vast majority of spaniels and retrievers can be trained to extremely high levels of per-formance without using the eCollar, we also recognize there are some really wonderful dogs that could not be trained without using it.

The best use of the eCollar in the flushing dog world is to spot fix problems that simply cannot be solved by any other means–but should not be used as a day-to-day training tool. To train a flushing dog us-ing an eCollar requires an incredibly soft touch. For example both of us have witnessed the new phenomenon known as the "creeping" or soft flush. This is directly attributable to the use of the eCollar in steadying to flush and shot. The dog, fearful of being zapped for flush-ing out of control, creeps up on the bird. However, retriever trainers use the eCollar quite effectively for training a relatively thick-skinned retriever with a personality to match. Our recommendation is to leave the eCollar use to a professional you know, trust, and who has exten-sive experience using the collar to help a dog over a rough spot in his training.

TEN

Concluding Thoughts and Parting Shots

The goal of this book has been to help you train your flushing dog for a fun-loving life at home or in the field with you, your family, and your friends under the daily trials and tribulations of city life. We sincerely hope we have succeeded in this goal. If you follow the approach we discussed in this book, you have a good chance of obtaining a well-trained dog in a period that is in direct proportion to your investment of time. A trained field-bred spaniel or retriever is a wondrous thing to view in action, but we all recognize this will be only a small part of your dog's life and your life as well.

Perspective is perhaps the most important word in this book. Keeping gun dog training in *perspective* is a tremendous challenge. The deeper one goes into the world of gun dogs, the tougher this becomes. Dogs are not robots; they are not automatons; they are not people. Dogs, quite simply, are dogs. With a nod to feline fanciers, dogs are arguably the closest creatures to humans in terms of day-to-day living and affections. Dogs live with us, love us, try our patience, entertain us, and generally make us appreciative of life. Life is short for dogs and us. It is easy to become a training, hunt test, or field trial junky–to take it all far too seriously.

Our parting advice is to enjoy your dog and make the most of your time with him. Hunting or just being outdoors with your canine companion are significant rewards; ones that should be enjoyed to their fullest extent. Enjoy the dog games for what they are–an off season pastime to help keep your dog's skills sharp and a chance to mingle with people who share your interests. Perhaps atypical for authors, we took our own best advice. As a special treat this year, we packed up dogs, kin, shotguns, food, and libations and made a beeline together for the pheasant country of South Dakota. The dogs performed superbly (not flawlessly) and we only wished our shooting was the equal of the dogs (we did get our limits every day). We hope you decide to do the same.

Tony Roettger, Chip Schleider, Alexander Schleider, Lynn Campbell, Phlatlands Northern Skye MH WDX and Dardnell Denby Of Windmillwood WD and 2003 runner-up High Point Cocker Puppy in the U.S. after a wonderful pheasant hunt in South Dakota.

BIBLIOGRAPHY

Kenneth C. Roebuck, *Gun-Dog Training: Spaniels and Retrievers*, Stackpole Books, 1982

Pamela Owen Kadlec, *Retriever Training for Spaniels*, Just Ducky Press, 2002

Joe Arnette and George Hickox, *Training Retrievers and Spaniels to Hunt 'Em Up*, Silver Quill Press, 2000.

James B. Spencer, *Retriever Training Tests*, 2nd Edition, Alpine Press, 1997.

D. L. and Ann Walters, *Training Retrievers to Handle*, 1979.

Joe Irving, *Training Spaniels*, Swan Hill Press, 2002

James B. Spencer, *HUP! Training Flushing Spaniels the American Way*, 2nd Edition, Alpine Press, 2002.

Keith Erlandson, *The Working Springer Spaniel*, Excellent Press, 1995.

Charles Fergus, *Gun Dog Breeds: A Guide to Spaniels, Retrievers, and Pointing Dogs*, June 1992)

Julia F. Gascow and Edward K. Roggenkamp, *The New Complete English Springer Spaniel*, 4th Edition, Hungry Minds, Inc, 1994.

ABOUT THE AUTHORS

ANTHONY Z. ROETTGER. Tony Roettger is a well-known professional gun dog breeder and trainer specializing in English cocker and English springer spaniels. His dogs have won and placed in numerous field trials. He and his wife Bethann own and operate Roettger Ridge Kennels in North Branch, Minnesota. He is a frequent contributor to magazines on gun dog training.

BENJAMIN H. SCHLEIDER III. Chip Schleider is an amateur gun dog trainer, marketing executive for a large aerospace company, and retired Army officer with a Ph.D. in International Studies from the University of South Carolina. He, his wife Catharine, and son Alexander live in Great Falls, Virginia; his oldest son, First Lieutenant Christian Schleider, is serving with the United States Army. Chip often contributes to gun dog training magazines and he is an avid hunt test enthusiast.

INDEX

Index